The Prop

Also by Steve Rhodes

The God Code

Steve Rhodes

The Prophecy of Ra Uru Hu

RME
LONDON
baantu.com

First published 2012 by
RME
London
United Kingdom

Fifth Edition (rev 1.0)
published 2017

Copyright © by Steve Rhodes
Steve Rhodes asserts the moral right to be
identified as the author of this work.

ISBN 9781549886461

This book is copyright material and must not be copied, reproduced, transferred, distributed, leased, licensed or publicly performed or used in any way except as specifically permitted in writing by the publishers, as allowed under the terms and conditions under which it was purchased or as strictly permitted by applicable copyright law. Any unauthorised distribution or use of this text may be a direct infringement of the author's and publisher's rights and those responsible may be liable in law accordingly.

Editor: Stephanie Sprague

Visit **baantu.com** to find more out about the author and any news.

Disclaimer:
This book is designed to provide information and motivation to our readers. It is sold with the understanding that the publisher is not engaged to render any type of psychological, legal, or any other kind of professional advice. Neither the publisher nor the author shall be liable for any physical, psychological, emotional, financial, or commercial damages, including, but not limited to, special, incidental, consequential or other damages. Our views and rights are the same:
You are responsible for your own choices, actions, and results.

A wonderful fact to reflect upon, that every human creature is constituted to be that profound secret and mystery to every other.

—Charles Dickens

The Encounter

Ra first had no other way of thinking about this story other than as a story about madness. It wasn't normal. It wasn't even normal according to the way in which most revelations take place. Because of his own natural scepticism, it was easy for him not to tell the story of his "encounter" for many years; it was mad and there was no proof. That's what's so interesting about telling stories.

He was already mad anyway. By any standards of society, Ra was already mad even before the encounter. At the time, he was living wild in the hills of the Mediterranean island of Ibiza and very much alone in a process that he didn't even try to understand. He had gone along for the ride; not thinking about what was happening to him because it was frightening. He assumed he had lost it, whatever that meant. It was his mid-life and he was aware enough of how things worked. What surprised him about his craziness was that it was entertaining. It was the most interesting thing that had ever happened to him: to go crazy and get away from everything that defines Western civilisation.

It was January the 3rd, 1987. He was living in this extraordinary old ruin, what the locals call a ruina. It had been built hundreds of years ago and was sitting over a dry cistern over a former water well. The original front door and most of the house had collapsed long ago and was no more than an entrance, an archway, to what now appeared to be a courtyard. The household ran out of water about two hundred years ago and if you ran out of water back then you couldn't stay in such a dwelling. You wouldn't be able to grow anything to survive. The building had deteriorated slowly over time. Ra first saw the ruina in 1984 when he rented the main house called *C'as Coxtu* down below from the people who owned the whole property. This was a few years before his days of living wild. The landlord had turned the ruina into some kind of guest room for the main house, a very simple, small, enclosed place. All that was left from the original house was that one room. The rest were all broken down walls. It was not very pretty, but it was functional.

He had a friend who was an English poet who once had no place to live. Ra told him that he could come and live in this ruina, back when he himself was still renting the main house. Some time later, when Ra stepped out of his life and left everything behind, the poet would return the favour. The poet came to Ra one day and said: "I have a place for you to live. You should really get off the ground. You've been on the ground too long. Why don't you come and live in this ruina that you gave to me? I have to go to England anyway." And so that's how he ended up in this strange place.

The ruina had this big, huge, wooden door that opened with one of those giant, iron skeleton keys, a very old-fashioned 19th century key. Many years before he had even heard about Ibiza, he used to doodle all the time. And what he used to draw was this key. Over and over again. Around the time that his daughter was born, he used to draw in diaries. They were symbol diaries of his life and contained no words. They only contained drawings. On every single page, there was a drawing of this key and eventually he ended up having this key in his hands, living in the room that this very key opened the door to.

It was getting dark. It wasn't late, as it gets dark early in January on Ibiza. Ra was on his way back to the ruina. He had just received a free meal, which was always a treat for him because he didn't eat often in those days. He was mostly muscle and bone, not much else. There was a Dutch couple, fascinated by his life, which was considered quite notorious and even dangerous to some. This Dutch couple was merely fascinated with him and would come once a week to collect him. They would bring him to their house, would turn on their tape recorder, and let him talk. Ra would talk about what he was going through and then they would give him a nice lunch, some Pesetas, and send him home. It kept him alive.

The morning of that particular day, he had an enormous pain in his mouth, a toothache. The couple offered him something homeopathic, which had no effect on him, and afterwards drove him back to the main road closest to his ruina. He began walking up the side of the hill, coming from this road on a little path worn out from his footsteps up to the ruina, when his dog Barley Barker, a semi-wild creature, picked up his scent and came running down the hill to meet him. Barley was savage. He was a natural-born killer. He had a master that never fed him, because he himself never had any food. Barley had to feed himself so he would hunt sheep. He knew Ra from the moment he was two days old, when he was given to him by a friend's daughter. The dog knew his scent and liked him, but not many other people. Ra watched him one day kill another dog in a dog fight. It was brutal. The moment Ra had stepped onto the path to the ruina, Barley could already feel him. Given Ra's life at the time, he had a deep connection to animals, and so after Barley came and said hello, they started walking together towards the ruina.

It only had one room, very simple and maybe two-and-a-half by five meters. There was a platform in it on which he slept. If he opened the door he would immediately see it. There also was a desk made out of some bricks with a board on top, and a chair. One wall was covered by shelves; the left-hand side with all kinds of books, the right-hand side with jars of herbs. All of this belonged to his friend, the poet. Also in the room were some masks made by a French artist, Pascal, a local from the island. He used to make hanging butterflies that people bought in the markets, and so there was a box of all of his stuff in there as well. Over the sleeping platform hung a kerosene lamp, but it was bone dry. The only place to get kerosene was from the other end of the island. Since Ra had neither money nor transportation, it was usually dark at night in the ruina, apart from the odd candle every once in a while. He was an Aries, and he lived his life like one. He got up with the Sun, and when it went down, he went to sleep. And that was what he was about to do when he was heading back to the ruina, sleep.

The ruina came in sight and there was a light underneath the door. When the two of them arrived, seeing that light underneath the wooden door, he got a funny feeling. Just that odd feeling. Actually, he could already feel a tightening in his stomach muscles before the light came into sight and he could tell that it bothered the dog, too. Barley usually led the way, but now he was behind him. There was only one key for the ruina and Ra had it in his hand; the old-fashioned one that nobody else could have had – and the door was locked. There was no other way in. Nobody would have bothered anyway. He was considered the local madman after all. Nobody would come near him. It was spooky.

Darkness had settled, turning the night really black. The sky began to fill with millions of stars. He was now very close to the door and he shouted at it. He shouted with a first taste of irony: "Who is there?" – There was no answer. The ruina sat on a hill that went down into a valley. On the other side, there was a whole ring of hills. So in this moment, in the dark, with this strip of light under the door, he heard his own voice echoing through the valley. "Who is there?" (*Hu is there*)

Tense, he put the key into the door. What happened then was not sequential. It was a kind of action-synthesis that he could later deconstruct into components, but it was not the same as what it was to experience it. He unlocked the door and pushed it inwards to the left with his hand. The kerosene lamp was lit and it was spinning clockwise over his bed. It was the first thing he noticed. At the same moment, his dog Barley crossed the threshold of the doorway. As he did so, he fell like a creature that had been shotgunned at close range. There was this sudden pressure in Ra's head and in this moment of pressure Ra heard a voice. It wasn't pleasant; the voice of a cigar smoking, 155-year-old woman. A dark, hard, cold, frightening voice with a flavour of intelligence that he did not recognise. And as he heard that voice – as the dog crashed and the lantern spun – his body exploded with water. It was gushing from his head, arms, legs and groin. There was literally a pool of body water on the floor. The physical sensation of super-fast dehydration is pain. And in this emergence of the pain was this voice. And it said: "Are you ready to work?"

It was not a question. It really wasn't. The dog was lying on the ground in this pool of water and the Voice commanded to move it out of the way, so Ra dragged the dog under his desk where he would be for eight days. It would never move, it didn't seem to be breathing. And then he closed the door.

If you had ever told Ra what to do, chances were that he would never pay attention to you again. He spent most of his adult life being an arrogant man, somebody who demeaned the intelligence of others. He respected no authority. But here he was, in a situation where he was almost like an obedient dog. A frightened one. He felt like he had been running a marathon with nothing to drink. Every single muscle of his body had begun to cramp. It's hard to describe the intensity of such pain. Pain is relative after all. But he had never known anything so painful in his life. His body was violated. He was in agony and he felt like he had been raped. All of it occurred so quickly, and there was a moment when he assumed that he was about to die. But then something very strange happened. There was a sensation that started in his right hip. The best way to describe it would be an "energy suit". It started in his hip and moved both up and down at the same time. It felt like when your foot falls asleep and goes numb. This energy suit did not eliminate the pain, but it made it bearable. For the eight nights and days that followed, he couldn't touch or feel his skin. And then the Voice told him to do things.

There was a butane stove in the room with two little burners. The first thing he had to do was to light a fire on it. As he started the fire on the stove, the hair began to go up on his neck. A neon-blue light – about two inches in diameter – suddenly hovered in the middle of the room. The Voice said to follow the light. Throughout his earlier de-construction period of living wild Ra had worn a mufti headdress and there was also a Buddha shroud that somebody brought to him from Burma that was hanging on the wall. The light went over to the Buddha shroud, so he put it on. Then it went over to the library and pointed out three books. The King James Version of the New Testament, the Bhagavad Gita, and a Stanford University biology textbook. Under instruction, he placed all these things on the platform. There was a woven chessboard made out of leather, and a coil of copper wire that was used by the artist who made the butterflies. Ra had to gather all these various things and place them on the platform together with the books.

Then he was told to take herbs from the shelves – and he had absolutely no idea what was in these jars. The guy living there was some sort of herbalist, scouring all over the island for all kinds of different roots and herbs to make these strange concoctions. The light would move to specific jars, and Ra was told to put the herbs directly on top of the fire so they would burn. Slowly, the room began to fill with smoke. Then he had to put on one of Pascal's masks that were in the room.

A cracked mask, right down the middle, across the nose. It was quite a scene of madness.

So, there he was, sitting cross-legged on his platform, wearing a Buddha shroud over his head and a cracked mask in a room full of smoke from burning herbs. In front of him were the chessboard, the coil, the books and all the other items he had to gather.

And then, the strangest thing of all – the light went to the very top of the book case, over on the right, where there appeared to be an orange crate. He had to climb up on the desk to reach it and pull it down. Inside, there were half-made, big butterfly wings. The light went into the box and swooped down to the bottom to a bedding of newspaper. He reached down and pulled it out. It was a local publication from the Mallorca Daily Bulletin. On the front page was the story of the Mexican earthquake that had taken place in December 1986, just before the encounter. There was the story of a fellow, Israel Diaz, trying to dig out his pregnant wife from underneath the rubble where she had to stay for eight days. It was a story of how he rescued her, saving her together with the baby. So, Ra took the front page of this newspaper and placed it on top of the whole conglomeration of things on his bed. At the foot of it, he had a few Ray charts he was investigating from his late study of theosophical thought. There were all these charts that he had drawn up from people he knew. The Voice told him to get one of these charts, specifically of a man who was an acquaintance, and to put it on the fire. Ra put it on top of the smouldering herbs and went back to sit on the platform.

All of a sudden, he heard voices. It was very strange. He

heard Spanish voices in particular, so he couldn't understand what they were saying. Ra was too astonished by what he was looking at anyway: a piece of paper on top of flames, but not burning. And while it wasn't burning, there were all of these sounds, like voices and noises. At some point, he became very tired and was given the first of three mantras he would receive. He had no idea what it meant. After repeating it a number of times, the paper exploded into flames and disappeared. Exhausted, he fell back onto the platform. He felt like he was levitating; his body couldn't feel the platform at all. Then the Voice began to teach him.

It was wonderful, because when it spoke he had no pain. He was just floating in an "information field". The Voice gave him the story of the Big Bang, which it called the story of the Consciousness Crystals and the nature of being. He had never heard anything like it. He was silent. He had never known himself to be so silent. It was all so very strange. Outside it was raining. As a matter of fact, it was more than raining. It was pouring rain. Ra remembers floating through the night, not awake and not asleep. He couldn't sleep with the pain, not that he thought he could have slept anyway. He had no hunger and he had no thirst. Eventually, when the morning light came, the Voice said that there was somebody at the door and that he should open it. There were two people standing there. An Englishman and his girlfriend from India. It was *his* chart that he had burnt on the fire.

The Englishman had this deeply confused look on his face,

because the two of them had been on their way from the island to France, already having crossed the sea by ferry, when they had suddenly felt compelled to see Ra, not knowing why and came back. So they were standing in the doorway, and the Voice told Ra to let them in, and so he did. It was very odd. She sat in the chair beside his dog, the one that didn't move and didn't breathe, never noticing. The Englishman sat on the other end of the platform from him. Then the Voice said to Ra to tell them about the Consciousness Crystals.

Afterwards, the Voice tricked Ra. It said to Ra: "Tell the Englishman that you can give him the Crystal that belongs to him." Ra had to tell them to come back that very evening for this. Then the Voice told Ra to throw them out, and that's what he did.

When he closed the door, he went over to the desk and was about to get his first taste of what would be the concrete magic of his encounter. He drew a *Graph*. It was an incredible experience. He couldn't feel the pencil in his hand. And here was this strange thing, whatever it was, describing to him how to do this, how to draw it, where to put everything, the numbers, all of it.

That night they came back, just as they were told to do. Ra invited them in and closed the door. The girlfriend went over and sat down by the desk as before, and the Englishman and Ra sat on the platform. Ra again put on the shroud with the cracked mask and gave him the other mask. Then he put the herbs on the fire, as he did the day before, and the room filled with smoke.

Ra had absolutely no idea what he was doing. He was caught in this incredible movie without choice. The Englishman was looking at Ra, wondering what was going to happen, but Ra had no clue. Ra had told him that he was going to get the Crystal he deserved, but he had no clue what that even meant. As he could feel the tension rise, all of a sudden, out of the Englishman's right ear came a light. A small, vibrating and three-dimensional white light. It went straight up into the air and came directly over Ra's head and went into it. The moment it went into Ra's head, the Englishman began to vomit. Not just retching, but things started pouring out of him unlike anything Ra had ever seen. He felt an incredible rush of adrenaline. Then the Voice told Ra to send them away.

The woman got up and went out of the door, but the Englishman couldn't move and was still vomiting. Ra grabbed the bed cover that the Englishman was on, and yanked him on it, literally dragging him out, throwing him into the puddle outside the front door of the ruina and slamming the door behind him.

About three years later, Ra met this man again and the man claimed that Ra had stolen his mind. As a consequence, he had been institutionalised for a number of years.

When Ra entered into this experience, his name was just Ra. After the event he would be *Uru Hu*, which is a title given to him by the Voice. *Uru* is this white light that entered him. If he closed his eyes, he could see it. He continued to see it all these years since then until he died. The light moved. He and the light communicated. It's one of those magical things about the Mandala Wheel and the placement of the Gates. Ra didn't do any of that. Uru did. It was a strange thing to live with, and Ra had no idea what it was. It wasn't like the light was telling.

When the Englishman and the girl left, the Voice got serious. Ra could remember sitting with his back to the wall on the platform, very confused by this white light in him. In his panic, he suddenly felt something taking and moving him. His head was snapped back, as far as you can imagine. It was so far back that there was practically no air going through, and in that moment three more lights went directly into his body. He had never been shot, but imagined that's what it probably felt like. Right there, he thought he was going to die. There was no way he could survive this. He could not breathe, and he had this incredible pain in his chest from the penetration. He could feel these things, whatever they were. He could feel them inside of him, not knowing what they did. And he would never find out if they ever left. All he knew is that it was incredibly painful. When it was over, he floated, not touching anything. He closed his eyes and watched this light, realising that it was responding with *yes* and *no*, in form of up-down movements, and circular movements.

Eventually, he and the light would go further than that, finding a real way to communicate. For years after the encounter, he always thought it would go away. Whatever its purpose was, it never told him what to do and the communication was always deeply limited. Ra later lived the patina of a relatively normal life after the experience. Having a family, doing constructive, good work in the world, and at the same time having this strange thing inside that always had something to say.

The third day was a horrid day, and he remembered feeling it before he saw it. But the nights had been bizarre, too. He couldn't sleep and yet he never was fully awake either. So when the light came on the third day, he sort of got a grip on what was going on. He felt so odd, and when he opened his eyes, trying to focus, he realised he had no skin. He was covered in scales. He had no genitals. If you want to know what panic and shock is, that was the moment. One could only wonder if the scales would ever go away and the genitals return. It was horrifying like some kind of reptilian science-fiction creature. The scales would eventually disappear. It took hours, but then suddenly they were gone. His body had returned.

That night, the Voice took him outside into the courtyard. There was this cracked piece of mirror, and Ra had to stand in front of it. He was given a magic mystery tour of past lives. All kinds of images. There were these smoky, hazy faces, one after the other. It wasn't like he was given stories. Every once in a while he got a funny feeling, looking at a face. What he was shown were all the past lives of his Personality Crystal in this *Round*, which must have been hundreds of them. It went on for too long. It was frightening how many of them there were. Ra later said that it was boring, given the intensity of everything else. He never really had any sense of past lives or a particular interest in them. In fact, he never enjoyed it when the Voice told him about himself. It had been much more entertaining surviving the experience than dealing with the madness of being told that you were this and that.

The Voice never told him what to do with this knowledge or what the experience was for. It was kind of obvious he had guessed. The entire experience was amazing and confusing at the same time. He felt like someone with multiple personalities.

For example when he had the experience of being taught about the Graph, all of the Centres suddenly had voices. They were all talking to him from inside his body, from his own Centres. Very strange, and rather frightening. All these voices inside: male, female, young and old, arguing and talking over each other.

People have always wondered how he had received the information, because the amount is staggering. I guess the only way one can describe it is that some of it was planted in him.

He never said much during those eight days and nights. The Voice responded to two thoughts of his that barely made it to the surface. One of them was his concern for his dog, and the other was his amazement at the information. He wanted to know where it was coming from and the Voice said: "From the Book of Letters."

Many years afterwards, on tour in the United States, a woman came up to him, telling him about a friend of hers. He had gone mad in January 1987 and remained institutionalised ever since. The last thing he did was write in his journal: *From the Book of Letters*. He never wrote anything again.

How Ra received the information can also be explained as that he was closest to the source. The ruina sat over an empty cistern and it was into that cavern that the Design Crystal bundle came. It's not what other messengers have connected to in the past. They usually connect to Personality Crystal bundles. What he received came from the totality of the form principle. He was sitting on top of it, taking it in through the neutrino stream and Aura contact.

He was told a lot, wonderful things and mysterious things. He was shown things and heard things. When he was looking back, years later, he realised how incredible it was, what a privilege it was to have such a strange experience, but back then, he was just tired of the pain.

The end was beautiful, as ends should be. It was the eighth day and the Voice told him to go up the mountain above the ruina, a very beautiful and isolated place with a stunning view. So he went up there and sat down. It was around midday and the Voice told him that it was leaving. Then it said the strangest thing to him. It told him to stare straight into the Sun. It was kind of a joke that he was so upset about the idea of staring into the Sun after all the madness that he has been through, but he was. He assumed that he would be blinded. The Voice gave him the last mantra and said: "Your name is Ra, and it's your *dog*, so look at it"

So he sat there and opened his eyes to the Sun. And as he did that, the Voice was gone.

What an incredible experience to look into the Sun with a full stare, and have the light burn through his eyes, down into the oesophagus. It's a burning sensation like what it feels like when you take a quick shot of whiskey. It burns down into your stomach and literally sets it on fire.

It's when he saw the mystical Blue Angel, this incredible blue form that emerges, dancing with the pulse of the Sun. When you look into the Sun, it's alive. You don't notice when you're just walking in the world. You can't see it breathe. And when look at it totally, completely without fear, you see that it's alive – breathing and pulsing. You can almost sense the consciousness of it.

He sat there for hours. And at some point he stood up and slowly began to walk down the hill. As he did so, racing up to greet him, was Barley. Eight days. No movement, no breath, no food, no liquids, and there he was, bouncing along and wagging his tail.

It was over and he was not relieved. He thought he would have been. You only have that kind of magic if you are lucky once in a hundred lifetimes; to step out and go beyond the veil. A great nihilist like himself, meeting the forces. It was wonderful. And how depressing it was to come back into the world. To be a freak in that world. To have nothing. To have all this knowledge and to have nothing.

After the encounter he experienced depression for the only time in his life, because it's not the kind of story that you want to tell too many people. It's an odd story, and given the way our culture operates it's even frightening to some people because they tend to project on it something it is not. Going through such an experience, being in such a space, and then leaving it? It's painful. You crawl back into your mundane body, and you realise that it has weight and form; that it has to eat, and that the world is full of fools. You are not exactly going to run around telling people that "a voice" told you how the universe works.

He was kind of feeling sorry for himself, not something he had ever done before. He was already an incredible freak, living a freak's life. He had no money and no home. He thought he had his moment of exhilaration, and that was the end of it. So now he basically tried to get rid of it, but he couldn't. He burnt everything, all the notes, but it wouldn't go away. For about nine months afterwards, he floated in a sedated world, trying not to be Ra Uru Hu.

There were physical differences before and after the encounter. His own mother didn't recognise him, didn't recognise his eyes. The texture of his skin and his voice changed. The nature of his laugh was different. There were many physical changes in his body that were easily recognisable by people who knew him. But the most obvious change is the one that we see in the body of his work. Ra knew that he was kind of smart, but never a genius. The years that followed after the encounter, however, were occasionally nothing but genius. That's not him. That was Ra Uru Hu, and not Robert Krakower.

The child in the womb of that wife in the Mexican Earthquake was carrying a Crystal. This was not a Crystal that typical human beings would carry. The English visitor during the event was a mule. He must have received it in France from somebody else before he felt compelled to come back and fulfil his task. They were both caught up in the drama without any choice. The Englishman is fine now and lives in Amsterdam.

The only concern that Ra had about the story of the encounter was that it might make him, the person, more interesting than the knowledge itself. The cult of personality is a dangerous thing. There are a lot of people who would love to turn this story into religious spirituality, and there are others who will project that it is dark, bad and the devil's work.

Others will think it is just a story, even maybe something he made up. It was always a strange story for him to share anyway. But however bizarre it is, he thought it was a story that needed to be told. He always said so himself: he is either the strangest guy on Earth or just whacking crazy. The truth is probably something we will never know.

The Design of Humans

The Crystals and the Monopole

All humans possess a Design Crystal, a Personality Crystal and a Magnetic Monopole.

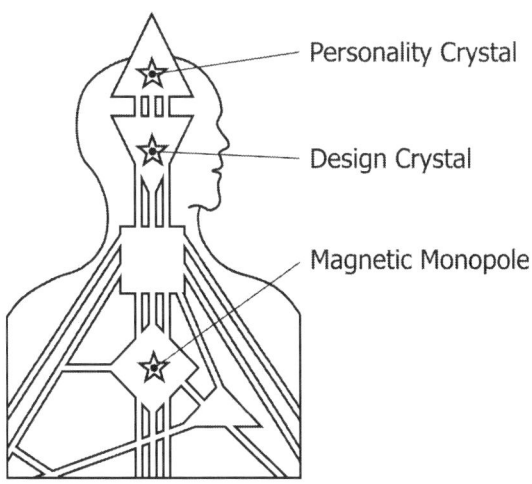

The two Consciousness Crystals are tiny in size. They are slightly bigger than a neutrino, which is an incredibly small particle to begin with. We call them "Crystals" in order to understand their characteristics and principles.

They are not really Crystals. But it helps to understand the shattering, the filtering and the Fractal aspects. They are what science understands as dark matter, and it's through them that we filter information, that we filter consciousness out of the neutrino ocean. Every Crystal is unique in shape and, therefore, must filter information in a unique way. Through that filtering, it actually produces more information. It's a two-way process. We receive information and we also send out information that has been altered by going through our Crystals. This is how the consciousness program that governs the universe writes itself. It's a never-ending cycle. So, when people think that there's this great intelligence at work and that there must have been some superior mind, it's not true. We are *it* and it is *us*. And it's evolving. We are the co-creators of the consciousness-field. We do it all the time, and for 14 billion years now, even when we sleep.

At the time of our conception, the Design Crystal began to build our body in our mother's womb. It is connected to the brain. After approximately six months, the body has developed far enough for the second Crystal, the Personality to come in and exactly 88° to the Sun later (approximately 3 months) you are born.

The Personality Crystal is connected to our mind. It is what some might call our "soul", the eternal part of us that incarnates over and over again in form. It is what gives us our characteristics or "personality".

When a Personality Crystal is out of form (not incarnated), it resides within the Earth's atmosphere, above ground. Personality Crystals reside in bundles when out of form. There are many Crystal bundles around the Earth, and some of these bundles are so massive in size in terms of Crystal numbers that it's not even possible to imagine such a number. What's interesting to know is that most of these Crystals never incarnate in form. We, the ones who do incarnate into human form, are only a small minority of these Personality Crystals. Kind of specialists.

When we look at the human incarnation process, first we have the Design Crystal that builds our body for approximately two-thirds of the human pregnancy before the neocortex is developed enough and ready to accept the Personality Crystal. This arrival of the Personality is where the illusion starts. This is where your life starts. It's also when the form becomes conscious.

Homo sapiens, which existed for over 100,000 years, was the first species that was conscious of its own existence, the first being that actually had a mind. There was no one there to be conscious of the illusion, of existence, of the universe, before that. Not even Neanderthals. The mind allows you to see existence relative to yourself.

Finally, we have the Magnetic Monopole, which is here to attract people and situations for us throughout our life. It is connected to the Love Centre, which is one of nine Pressure Centres that a human form possesses. It holds us together in the illusion of our separateness. It holds together the two Crystals, and arrived with the Design Crystal at conception, but most importantly, it controls what and who we love.

Initially, the Monopole was embedded into the Design Crystal. They both came from the single Design Crystal bundle that resides inside the Earth near its core. It's the Monopole that structures existence and holds together the illusion of what we think is us and our body. It holds together our Personality and Design Crystals in the illusion of being separate from everything else. It's the vanity of humans making them think they are in control of their lives, that *they* are the driver. They are not. It's an illusion. We are here for the ride.

The Graph

A body controlled through nine Pressure Centres is called Uranian body. From 2027 onwards, we will see the emergence of a species (parallel to ours) that will have a Uranian body, like we do, but is no longer human at all. This will be the "true" Rave. That's the actual purpose of us: to give birth to the Rave. We are not Rave. We are humans inside a Rave-like body. You could say we have almost a Rave body with a different internal wiring. A "human" wiring.

Evolution came up with a very clever solution to make the

emergence of the next species possible. It created a form that can house two species. The nine-centred Uranian body can house humans and Raves. Eventually, after tens of thousands of years, it will evolve into a form with 11 Pressure Centres, and humans will disappear, like Neanderthals did. This process will be cut short though, because life on Earth will probably end in approximately 1,300 years. But we are already at the threshold that marks the end of humans. We have already been robbed of the true human body and have to come to terms with living inside something that is not for us. We have to learn to adapt to the world of Raves.

If you want to see your own Graph, you can go to **baantu.com**. All you need is a precise date and time of birth to do this.

The Graph is the result of two calculations, based around two specific points in time. The calculation on the right is for the Personality Crystal and is based on your actual birth time. The calculation to the left is about the Design Crystal and derived from the time when the Sun was 88° earlier in the zodiac (approximately 3 months before). At these two different points in time, we look at the positions of 13 celestial bodies. They are: the Sun, the Earth, the Moon, the North and South nodes and eight other planets.

The Sun needs approximately 365 days to make a full circle around the zodiac, Pluto 248 years.

The Mandala Wheel

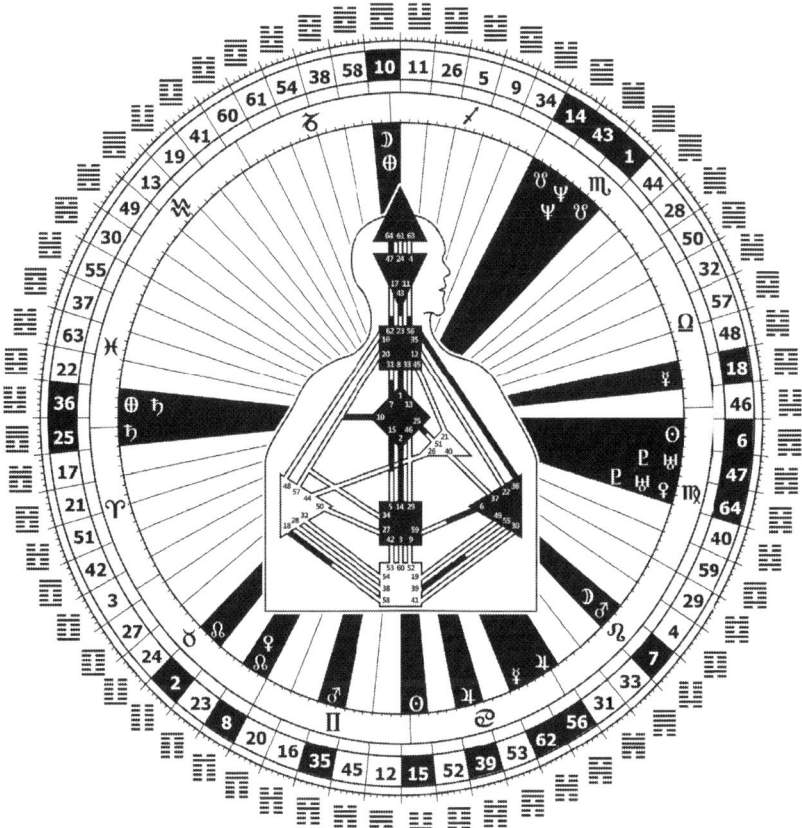

The ancient Chinese philosopher Shao Yung already used the circular arrangement of the 64 Gates, and the Kabbalist Marguerite de Surany had the them allocated to the zodiac, but probably not in the same way as the Voice told Ra Uru Hu.

The zodiac represents the plane (ecliptic) on which all planets move around the Sun, seen from Earth. When you look at the planets, Sun and Moon, they seem to move around the ecliptic, with the Sun taking a full year to return to the same position. The planets, moon and the Sun move counterclockwise around the zodiac, the nodes of the Moon in the opposite direction (clockwise). Since we watch the position of the celestial bodies in our Solar System relative to Earth (which itself rotates around the Sun), they can appear to move backwards at certain times, which is called retrograde movement (except for the Sun, which always moves forward).

The Mandala Wheel is divided into 64 Gates. Every Gate is assigned a specific position in the zodiac. You then calculate the positions of the planets both at the time of your birth (Personality) and the time when the Sun was 88° earlier (Design). You then insert all the celestial bodies at their correct position in the Mandala Wheel. Now, you can see what Gates are active in your Graph.

One Gate alone doesn't do much. It's a mere possibility for a full Channel. Only when we have both sides (Gates) of a Channel defined, we get an active Channel. The moment you have an active Channel, you automatically have a defined Pressure Centre on both ends of the Channel, influencing your activities in life.

What's important to understand is that you not only have the Channels of your birth design available (permanent pressure), but also additional Channels that the daily transit field and the connection with other people bring. You look where the 13 celestial bodies are at the moment (which Gates) and add them to your Graph. This is actually the pressure you feel at the moment. You can see the transit and other people's influences at **baantu.com**.

The Flow of Information

It all begins with a neutrino going through a Consciousness Crystal. What are neutrinos? The are incredibly tiny particles that have mass and travel almost at the speed of light. They go through everything: planets, humans, even a wall of lead, several light years thick (if such a thing would exist). But because neutrinos have mass, they also exchange information with the object they go through. Their oscillation changes.

Neutrinos get produced in stars and it's our Sun that provides us with 70% of the neutrinos on Earth. About 65 billion Solar neutrinos per second pass through every square centimetre perpendicular to the direction of the Sun. Neutrinos are carriers of information. They carry information throughout the universe. They connect everything. They don't connect everything randomly, but there is a special order – or you might call it hierarchy – in which information must flow in the universe. This is the how all the Crystals communicate with each other. They constantly receive and send information with the help of neutrinos going through them. We also call this hierarchy Fractal Lines and it has to do with how the two Crystals out of which the universe came into existence (the Baan and the Tu) shattered. If you were able to put all the pieces back together before the shattering at the Big Bang, you would see lines of fracture. And it's along these lines, that information flows. Everything in life happens along these fracture lines, that we also call Fractal Lines (not to be confused with fractal patterns).

Philosophically speaking, you could call the neutrinos the

ocean of consciousness in the universe, I call it the building plan. But neutrinos and the information they carry is only part of the story. The Crystals act like a decoder. It's not just decoding though. It's more like adding unique information to the neutrino when it goes through, It's why we call them Consciousness Crystals. They are actually the *creators* of the consciousness program. The stars only produce the medium to carry consciousness.

Every Crystal in the universe is unique in its shattering and quality. No two Crystals filter a neutrino in the same way. The actual information our mind and body receive, which you could call the blueprint of life, comes out of two components: the neutrino and your Crystals. These Crystals interpret the neutrino in a very specific way. They will also only listen to the correct information that is meant for them – information that has been going through other Crystals before. The Crystals that were close to ours before the shattering at the Big Bang are the important ones. The closer they were to us before the shattering, the more important their message is for us. The most important people that you will meet in your life, no matter if they are people giving you something or people that you pass things on to, are the ones carrying Crystals that were close to you before the shattering – people who are on your Fractal Line.

When the neutrino goes through the Crystal, it produces different "frequencies" influencing our behaviour.

The Crystal Bundles and the Incarnation Process

The *Design* Crystals that we humans, all other forms and all cells carry come from one single bundle residing in the centre of the Earth, near its core.

On the other hand, the *Personality* Crystals form a sheath around the Earth's atmosphere where they reside when not in form. The Personality Crystals form many bundles, not just one. For example, there is the Christ bundle, the Buddha bundle, and so on. In the beginning, there were only 16 bundles, according to the 16 Faces, but now there is an enormous number of them. You have to imagine a layer of Crystals that encircles the whole Earth. These bundles move through the atmosphere and can also move through rooms. All neutrinos have to go through these Consciousness Crystals first before they reach life on Earth. If you could look at Earth from a great distance and you could see these Crystals, you would not see the Earth. All you would see is that the Earth is literally encased in – what appears to be – a Crystal sphere. You would see one big Crystal.

The information that Ra received in his encounter came from the Design Crystal bundle that, as we already heard, usually resides in the centre of the Earth. He experienced it in the limitation of what it is to be human. His human form invented "the Voice". There is no way to explain some things other than in ways we can handle them. We describe things in the way we can, and we identify them in the best way in which we can, whatever they really might be. You can call a bundle a ghost, a demon, a spirit or an angel, but in reality it's part of the consciousness field of the totality.

Human Conception

At your conception, a Design Crystal from the bundle at the Earth's core and started to build your vehicle. At the moment of orgasm, the sperm carrying the Design Crystal, guided by its embedded Magnetic Monopole, finds and enters the egg in your mother.

Approximately three months before your birth, when your body was ready and the neocortex enough developed, the Magnetic Monopole called the Personality Crystal and it left a particular Personality Crystal bundle in the Earth's atmosphere. It will return to the same bundle after death.

Your Personality Crystal has been doing this over and over again, hundreds and hundreds of times, experiencing the different levels of form development. This path of experimentation, the suffering of humanity, and all the pain of going in and out, is to serve a greater purpose of the potential of a form that truly can house consciousness. It is a consciousness that we ourselves are not even capable of glimpsing.

Death

When you are dying, the Design Crystal re-unites with the Magnetic Monopole and together they then exit your body. This is the moment of your physical death.

Your Personality Crystal still stays connected to your mind when that happens. It is not yet released. There are still small pockets of oxygen in your brain that allow you to have self-reflected consciousness. The corpse still serves the Personality Crystal in order to complete its process. There is still activity in the brain.

Every human is supposed to go through a process after the moment of physical death to fully complete its incarnation. This can takes up to 72 hours after which the Personality Crystal finally gets picked up from its Personality Crystal bundle.

In order for a Crystal to reincarnate, the body must be left undisturbed for at least 72 hours. That probably means: no burial, no cremation, no removal of organs, no putting it under ground and no autopsy. Death does not liberate the Personality Crystal from the body. If it gets put under ground before 72 hours have passed, it might not be able to return to its original bundle. The Crystal will then "hang around" and will never be able to incarnate as human again. That is why today we have so many more than the initial 16 bundles from where we incarnated from.

It explains why the 16 Faces, the "gods", are losing their powers. They act as a Centre for the 16 original bundles, but now they are overwhelmingly outnumbered by the mutative bundles that have formed from Crystal that couldn't return, particularly over the last 500 years because of the population explosion. There are an enormous number of Personality Crystals that have been depleted from the original 16. The gods have lost their power. If you look at all the religions on Earth, the only ones that have managed to survive are the ones oriented on the Centre, monotheism. They are no longer paying attention to the 16 Faces, who have lost so much power and which ultimately will lead us to the closing of a door. The quality of information we receive is retarding. It's the ending of the Cycle of the *Cross of Planning*. In 2006, we have entered an age where innovation is going to die. In a sense, Sirius is bringing this, and Sirius is gone as we know. It's like a temple that's built on four pillars. You can knock out one pillar and for a certain amount of time that temple will try to find its balance, but at some point it will just collapse.

The Architecture of Life

The Inanimate

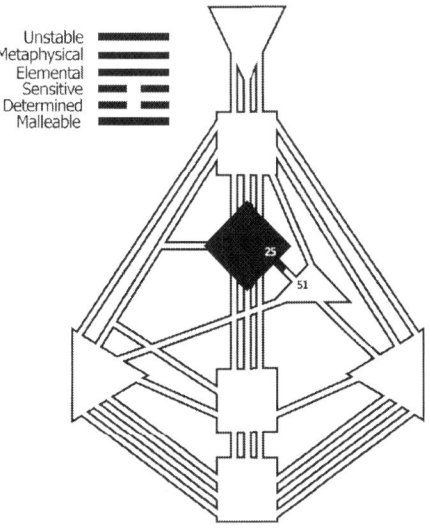

Unstable
Metaphysical
Elemental
Sensitive
Determined
Malleable

Plant

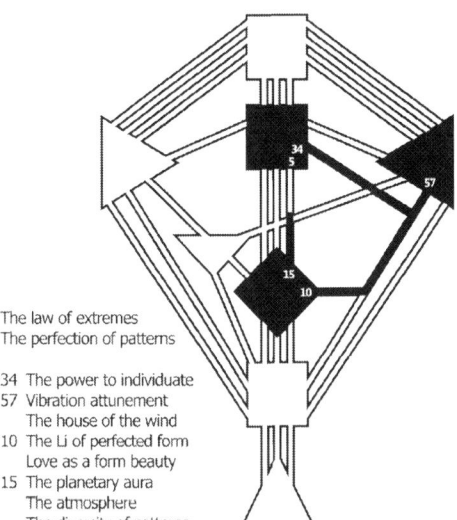

The law of extremes
The perfection of patterns

34 The power to individuate
57 Vibration attunement
   The house of the wind
10 The Li of perfected form
   Love as a form beauty
15 The planetary aura
   The atmosphere
   The diversity of patterns

The Cell

The law of organisation
The focused pulse

3 Mutation on/off switch
5 Pattern type
15 Rhythm growth rate

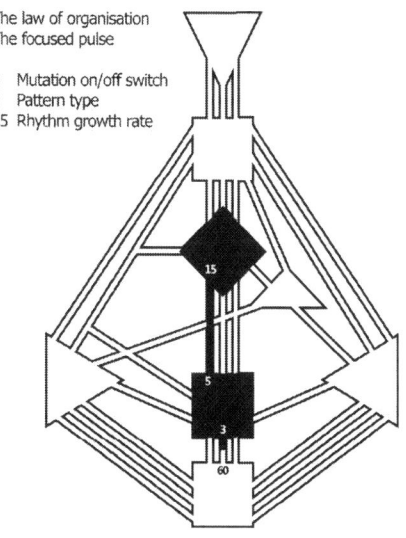

Insect

The law of no tomorrow
The rhythm of nature

20 The eternal now the hum
10 The penetrators
15 Vibration diversity
5 Fixing the collective pattern
34 The power to individuate
57 Vibration awareness

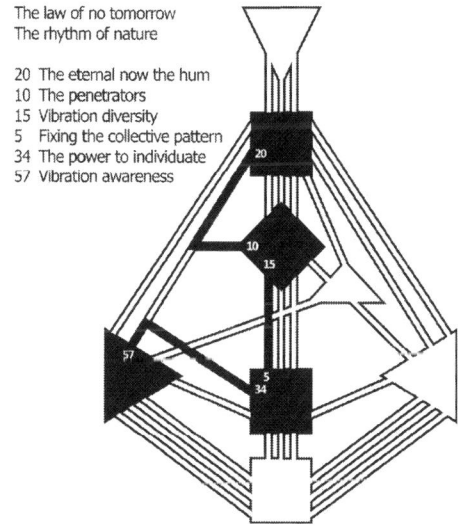

Bird, Reptile, Fish

The law of adaptation - direction through magnetism

44 Alertness - fear of being eaten
57 Acoustic clarity - fear of the unexpected
34 The power to proliferate
5 Collective fixed patterns
15 Extreme rhythms - magnetic harmony
1 Direction - unique expression
8 Imprinting

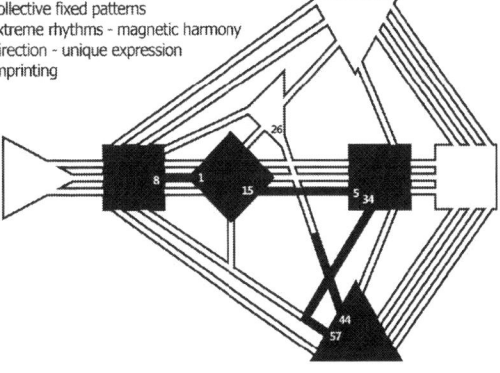

Mammal

Struggling for food and order in the now

19 The drive to find food
38 The fighter aggressiveness
28 The stalker listening intently
50 The herd instinct
27 Sexuality communal altruism
5 The fixing of patterns
15 Animal magnetism - the alpha

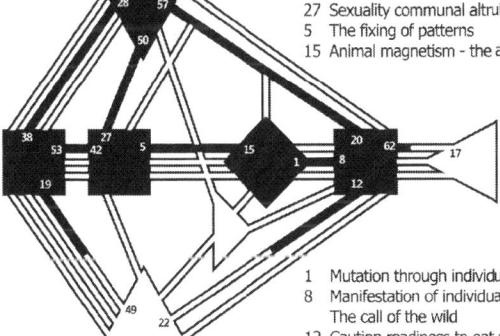

1 Mutation through individual direction
8 Manifestation of individuality
   The call of the wild
12 Caution readiness to eat or be eaten
62 Adaptation
20 Potential existential manifestation
57 Hearing in the Now
42 Power to mature through cycles
53 Mammalian vitality

The Story of the Consciousness Crystals

The Bhan & Tugh and the Beginning of our Universe

In the beginning, before the start, there were the two.
They have names.
Everything has a name.
One was called the Bhan, and one was called the Tugh.
They are the only link to what cannot be known.
They are of what is unknowable.
The rest, everything is the rest, is out of them.

The Bhan came from the outside, the Tugh was an egg.

The Tugh has always been inside.
Everything has always been inside.
The Outside of the universe is still inside.
These are the one that we possess as two.

Physicists have a problem. The theory of relativity and everything about how they understand the universe is based on the presence of light, but there had to be a moment before the light.

The Voice said that the totality is an unborn entity. It is alive. Ra called it poetically "the Child". We do not and cannot know what could possibly conceive such a thing. There is always a "ring-pass-not". The universe wasn't created at the Big Bang. It was already there. It was lying dormant. It was there before the Bhan came. It was there in the same sense that an egg can hang around and never get fertilised. The totality is an extraordinary illusion, a vast illusion that is a by-product of the juxtaposition of the Bhan and the Tugh from the beginning. Just the same as we are endowed with two Crystals. We are only the microcosm of this vast Program.

The Bhan and the Tugh are the only link to what cannot be known. The rest – and everything is the rest – is out of them.

Everything in the universe is moving away from each other, just like the foetus growing within the mother's womb. When we look at the universe, we are actually looking at an unborn entity from the inside. When we look at the stars in the sky, we look at the Child's body from the inside.

The Tugh had a cellular centre that carried anti-neutrinos, which then became neutrinos when you got to the Big Bang. The universe is built on a neutrino grid. Neutrinos are the most abundant particle in the universe, an estimated 40% of all matter. They have mass and travel nearly at the speed of light. When you look at the Tugh, you are looking at the prime Design Crystal that is going to be responsible for the entire form construct of what we call the universe.

The Bhan is a Design Crystal, too. The Tugh is yin and cellular, while the Bhan a little less yin. It is an organising Crystal. They are both Design Crystals and they are responsible for building the form. There is no yang. So in this Program, from the beginning, we're looking at two different kinds of Design form mechanisms. We're looking at one that is simply involved in all matter, the Tugh. And then, what we have coming from the outside is this ability – through the potential of the Bhan Crystal – to organise all of those Tugh Design Crystals through the neutrino field and to hold them together with the Magnetic Monopole. This is where the life Program really begins. The true Personality Crystal has not entered the Child, has not yet entered the totality, but we are very close to it. Our Personality Crystals in our bodies are in reality Design Crystals and act as a test-driver for the real single Personality when it will finally emerge in the Eron in around 200 million years. The Eron will be an almost eternal form that emerges after life on Earth has ended.

In the beginning there were only two Design Crystals. That shows you how densely we are part of what is a *form principle*. In the beginning there wasn't yin and yang. There was only yin and yin. When you look at the world now, you can see that the male of the species is simply an archetype of *imitation yang*. Such a wonderful joke!

In the beginning, before the start, there were the two.

Embedded in the Bhan was the prime Magnetic Monopole, which makes sense since it came from the outside. The moment you have a Magnetic Monopole you have a driver, and it knew exactly where to go.

Where this cosmology takes us is to the organisation of consciousness that is far beyond anything that we can manipulate, control, or interfere with. In other words, because we do not possess a true Personality, we do not possess a true mutative consciousness. There is no way that the grasp of the totality and the intricacy of the logic is something that we or any mind that's ever existed on this planet are capable of. In Ra's experience with the Voice, he was dwarfed by the consciousness field. Dwarfed isn't even the word! Beyond insignificant by just the power of that consciousness! We are not originators. We do not yet possess that potential, similar to the fetus that originates nothing within the womb. It doesn't. It is following a Program, a very predictable, in a way, Program. It's all laid out, in that sense, in the infrastructure of the original conception. It's chemistry and it's dynamics. This is us.

The Magic of Conception

A Rave has a Personality Crystal and a Design Crystal.
They are the same (Bhan).
The Bhan on the outside is a Design Crystal.
The Tugh is an egg.

The Personality Crystal of the Child has not yet entered the body.
Design Crystals are binary by nature.
The Tugh is "cellular", the Bhan is "prime".
When they met in the geometry they shattered.

When the Bhan and the Tugh met in the geometry, they shattered. This line of geometry stretches so far back it cannot even be dreamt. We are looking at an extraordinary compression that suddenly exploded and created enormous heat. If you could imagine the heat of the Sun, we would be talking about the heat of billions and billions of them. And the moment you have this heat, you also have light.

Each and every one of us is endowed with two shattered aspects of these Crystals. It is the shattering of the two prime Crystals that literally seeded the expanding universe, literally seeded it with its potential to receive and to filter the consciousness field.

Fractal Lines and the Centre

At the core of the Bhan was the prime Magnetic Monopole. Where it sits within the Child is the greatest of all mysteries, for that is the place of universal love and eternal oneness.

If you had looked at the Crystals a tiny fraction after the shattering, you would have seen the Fractal Lines. Each Crystal shattered in trillions and trillions of zillion pieces, but there is one piece that is called the Centre.

The Centre is not the middle, but it is the only Crystal that has the same basic characteristics as the whole Crystal before it shattered. Imagine holding the Crystal before the shattering to the light. It would cast the same light pattern as the Centre Crystal after the shattering. And out from the Centre, the Fractal Lines flow. What the Centre represents is a microcosmic Crystal that actually has the same potential as the whole.

All the Crystals that touched the Centre before the shattering, the very Crystals that surrounded the Centre, are on a first generation Fractal Line with it. These are the only Crystals the Centre can inform and impact directly. Information in the universe always flows down the Fractal Lines.

Crystals that touched the Crystals surrounding the Centre – touching the ones forming a layer between them and the

Centre – are second generation Fractal Lines, and so forth. So for example, if you meet someone in this life that is on a first generation Fractal to you, it means their Personality Crystal was touching yours before the shattering. If they are second Fractal Line, it means there was another Crystal in between you and them.

There is a hierarchy in the universe, but there is no place for vanity. There exists a law about how information must flow. Information always flows down from the Centre though all the Fractal Lines. You can only truly impact and be impacted by someone on your Fractal Line. And the closer someone is, the deeper the impact will be. This is something very important to recognise. You are always going to have either your deepest receptive impact or your deepest externalised impact on the other along that Fractal Line. Everything in our lives is always connected to that moment of the shattering; the Fractal Lines that formed in that very moment of it. Your mind can't see Fractal Lines and that's why it can't be trusted with everything.

Humanity has this vain concept of hierarchies, which goes back to the concept of most religions that small children are already brainwashed with. It's not the Crystals closer to the Centre (which they think is God) that are more important. It's always the Crystals that are closest to *you*.

Let's think about this in a three-dimensional way. If you shatter an object, it shatters in many directions. However, the shattering is not equal, not equal in the way that the Centre is not in the middle. So, for example, let's say the Centre is at the bottom end of an object. It means that some Fractal Lines are shorter than others. In other words, there will be long lines of Crystals that emerge through the long end, and less on the short end. Information flows down Fractal Lines. Let's say that I have some knowledge and you're on my Fractal. Then you receive the knowledge. You again have someone on your Fractal Line that receives the knowledge from you, and so forth, as long as the Fractal Line goes.

The thing to consider is that the information changes the further you move down the Fractal. It's clear that there may be a couple of dozen people on the planet who understood what Einstein was talking about. It's a very limited Fractal. By the time the Fractal is stepped down, eventually you have kids with T-shirts saying $E=mc^2$ and they know nothing about it. The original information is lost as it gets constantly changed down the Fractal, which is, in fact, not a loss of something but a transformation. It's how the Program, how consciousness evolves.

Every Crystal down the Fractal Line adds information according to its unique filter of consciousness. If you understand this, you see that the consciousness is not something that *emerges* from the Centre. There is no "all knowing" Centre or God. Consciousness is the *result* of the filtering of information down the Fractal Lines by all the individual Crystals. The last Crystal down a Fractal Line is as important as the Centre or anyone closer to the Centre. If your Crystal were to receive the information directly from the Centre, it would have no value for you. It needs to be processed by all the Crystals in front of it on its Fractal Line to the Centre in order to be of value to you. You can imagine the Crystals as decoders of information, of a data stream that we also call neutrinos, at the same time adding information according to your unique Crystal. All the Crystals together are the creators of consciousness of the universe, including yours.

You have to understand one thing: the Crystals that every one of us carry have been there from the beginning. If you would put back all our Personality and Design Crystals you would end up with the Bhan and Tugh before the shattering. We are all aspects of the whole. Unique, shattered aspects. So, if someone comes up to you one day and says to you: "I think you are an old soul!" You can reply: "And so are you!" Your Personality Crystal has been in existence for 14 billion years, and every single one is necessary to represent the whole. This is why there is no place for vanity. It is so clear.

After the shattering, you had the emergence of light, the electron, moving outward at the speed of light, in a way illuminating the darkness. The energy wave stripped away the vast majority of the Tugh aspects and as the movement reduced the heat, the energy began to freeze into form around Tugh cellular aspects. The first basic elements came into existence. The building of the cosmic body, the Child, had begun. The Tugh builds the body, the Bhan builds the brain of "the Child". Our Solar System is the centre of the cosmic brain, the Earth the place where the Design Crystal of the Child sits, until the beginning of the movement of the Crystal bundles in 1,300 years to Oberon.

Neutrinos – the Breath of Stars

Neutrinos are produced in stars, they are the source of consciousness. Neutrinos are a medium for consciousness, like data in a computer. But don't make the mistake of thinking the data that comes out of stars is *it*. It isn't everything. It's only when neutrinos pass through all the Crystals that we get to see consciousness as a whole. It's the passing of neutrinos through all the Crystals that creates consciousness in the universe. All the Crystals (including the ones you and I possess) add and change neutrino information according to their unique shattering aspect all the time, and by doing so create the whole. What emerges out of stars is only an aspect. It is only the beginning of a vast process. Seventy percent of the neutrinos we receive on Earth come from the Sun. We live in a very dense neutrino ocean. If we could see neutrinos, there wouldn't be anything else to see. From the Sun alone, 64 billion neutrinos pass through every square centimetre per second. Neutrinos carry the information that our Consciousness Crystals filter according to their unique aspects. These Crystals take in one neutrino at a time. Now you can understand why our Crystals are called Consciousness Crystals. Not only do they filter consciousness, but they themselves are creating it by altering the neutrino stream and adding their unique aspect, going out in all directions, at nearly the speed of light.

Only 4.6% of the universe is atomic. The rest is dark matter and dark energy. Neutrinos have mass (less than one millionth of an electron), travel almost at the speed of light, and pass through everything. By doing so, they exchange information with the Consciousness Crystals that are dark matter, when going through. They move into all directions. Through everything. It's the neutrinos that are the medium of the consciousness ocean we live in, and it's the Crystals that filter it. What they filter you can call "the Program". The Program that is building the Child. And all the Crystals in the universe are maintaining the Program by altering neutrino information all the time.

A wall of lead, a thousand light years thick, wouldn't slow down the neutrino. It goes through everything. It's quite something.

The neutrino with mass is literally the web, the ocean of information, that is binding together all forms, including us.

Stars

For more than two billion years the Monopole and the Design Crystal remained one.
Some stars are older than the beginning.
The Tugh and the Bhan did not meet in a vacuum.
They met on the inside and the inside was already there.
These are the stars of the wall.
One day, far away, when they begin to die, they will be the enemy. Until then, they are the Child's greatest allies.

Some stars are older than the beginning. There are stars that are older than the universe. The Tugh and the Bhan did not meet in a vacuum. There are stars on the wall. There is a connection between the universe and what the universe is part of on the outside, whatever that happens to be. And there are stars that control the entry point. If you want to see it in the context of mother and child – which is a very loose metaphor, so be careful with it – you are looking at the umbilical cord.

The Beginning Before the Start

There is a line of geometry that stretches so far back,
it cannot even be dreamt.
The shattered binary, held by the Monopole,
rides the incredible energy wave, holding to the line.

Compared to everything else racing out from the impact,
the bundle – mostly Bhan aspects
and the Magnetic Monopole – moved slowly.
The energy wave stripped away the vast majority
of the shattered Tugh aspects.
And as the movement reduced the heat,
the energy began to freeze into form
around the Tugh "cellular" aspects.
The first basic elements came into existence.
The building of the cosmic body had begun.

There is a line, a geometry, that far precedes the emergence of this universe. But for us, there will always be a ring-pass-not, a point in time or space where we can't go further, that is locked for us. That line is a line of neutrino string, which means that there is a programming agency of the consciousness beyond this ring-pass-not that touches us. It's always dangerous to say that, because it opens up a doorway for the finger of God to stick itself through the roof. Nonetheless, you don't have to see it in that way. What I do recognise is that the consciousness that is developing here is a consciousness that has been informed at its primary level by a much more ancient consciousness, a consciousness from before the start. So the string was always there. And it was there before the start.

Everybody has this trip about physics and cosmology, that somehow this is a miracle, that it all emerged out of nothing. It didn't emerge out of nothing. It's just that in terms of physics it's *nothing* because you can't see it, because you can only see things when there is light. When there is no light you don't see it.

The Bhan came from the outside. It had to come in. So, you begin to understand why the Bhan has a Magnetic Monopole. The moment that you have a Magnetic Monopole, you have a way of driving. You have the driver. You have the ultimate chauffeur that knows precisely where to go. It is the prime Magnetic Monopole embedded in the Bhan that knows where to find the Tugh.

From the beginning in this Program, we're looking at two different kinds of Design form mechanisms. One is the Tugh, which is simply involved in all matter and the neutrino potential, this inter-connectedness of all material. The other mechanism that we have is coming from the outside and has this ability to organise it through the potential of the Bhan Crystal; to be able to organise all of those other Design Crystals, to be able to organise them through the neutrino field, and to be able to hold them together with the Magnetic Monopole. This is where the life Program really begins.

Some Bhan aspects are ultimately going to take on the role of the Personality Crystal, or more precise "imitation" Personality. For example, the Personality Crystal we humans carry. And it's something else to understand: that all of the instruments of manipulating our consciousness field – and these instruments will include stars and moons – are objects that are endowed with Bhan Crystals. It is this Bhan, this potential to interface with the neutrino Program that gives us all of these thoughts, that brings us to this wonder about the nature of the consciousness field.

The Bhan

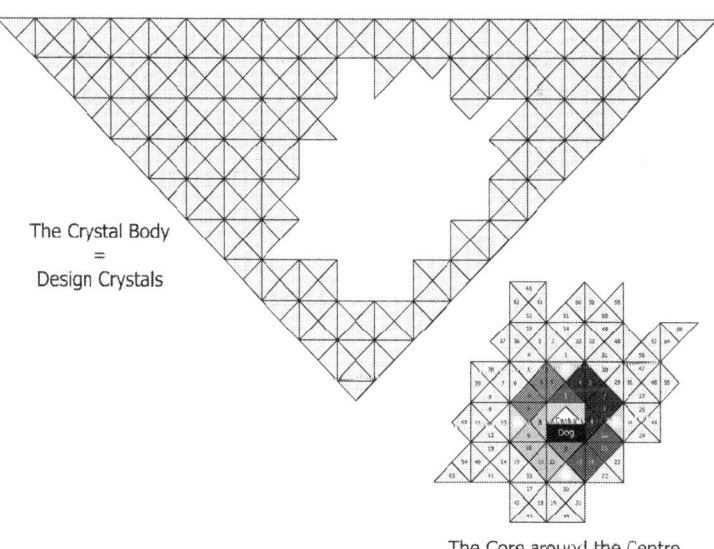

The Initiation of the Life Process

The Tugh and its anti-neutrino core are the builder
of the body of the Child.
The Program formula was compressed, dormant,
at the core before the start.
Then on impact, the race began.
First the light, piercing the darkness.
Then the string, close behind, laying out the lines.

Remember, the string was always there from before the start.
The shattering of the Tugh is the "forking of the paths".
This is the universe, variations of an image through
an infinitely shattered mirror.

Consciousness, awareness, love, direction – the forms out of which
it can all be experienced – this is out of the Bhan.
And the Bhan is not Yang. It is Yin.
Everything is Yin except the light.
And the light is an illusion.
The Tugh builds the body.
The Bhan builds the brain.
The Rave builds the temple.
The ark is empty.
We have not reached the place yet.

The phases of cosmic evolution are initiated in violent events.
The bundle, billions of years, guided by the Monopole, one with the
Design, in a movement towards the possibility of expressing love,
eventually reached its initiating place, meeting the star of the wall.
Love went away that day.
And that was the initiation of being.
When they meet again it is death,
darker than the Night of Brahma,
for it is death to the Child.

The bundle penetrated to the core of the star of the wall.
The cracking ripped apart the star.
The prime Magnetic Monopole was dis-embedded from
the prime Design Crystal as the Crystal itself shattered.
This is the birth of Rave Personality Crystals.
The Monopole was hurtled away from the mass,
caught in a cosmic spin.
When the Dervish dances, this is the celebration of the love,
which initiated consciousness.

For more than two billion years after the shattering, the Monopole and the Design Crystal still remained one. Eventually guided by the Monopole, they reached their initiating place by meeting the Star of the Wall. This is what initiated the shattering and disembodying of the prime Magnetic Monopole from the prime Design Crystal. It's another shattering that took place, this time of the Monopole. Here, we are looking at the beginning of the true form principle. Not cellular. That's already out there and expanding. You have the beginning of the programming agency. This capacity through this fractured Bhan Crystal and the shattered Monopoles to begin this process of controlling and programming; in that sense, the ultimate capacity of form to be endowed with consciousness. This is what it's all about.

Love went away that day. The Monopole and Design Crystal are truly one. And the moment that they separate is the moment that we become an act of love. We are not love. We cannot possess it, but we are the very by-product of it. We become the expression of love.

The Bhan had lost love and found form. Out of form the Design Crystal is dormant. In form it builds.

*The fragments of the core, all began to manifest
their individual aspects.
It was the dog for example that built the body of the Sun.
There were many other ingredients in the bundle
when it fused with the star.*

*The prime Magnetic Monopole before this event
could best be described as a cluster.
The power of the Monopole is to attract.
At this stage, all of its aspects – Monopoles in harmony
with the single prime Design Crystal – were as one.
When the Design Crystal shattered, the harmony was broken.
The law of the monopole is hold on to everything.
The shattering destabilised the Monopole cluster.
The spin was more powerful then the prime Magnetic Monopole's
capacity to keep the cluster together.
Every fragment of the shattered Design Crystal was seeded
with a Monopole aspect from the cluster.*

There is always Death and Rebirth

This disembodying of the Monopole from the Design Crystal is the initiation of being. When they will meet again it is death – darker than the Night of Brahma – for it will be the death to the Child. The Voice never said how long it will exist. It only said how long it would take to get to the point that it would emerge into the world beyond its own, whatever that means.

One can assume that maybe it will exist for tens or hundreds of billions of years – who knows – but at some point it too shall die. It doesn't matter about scale – there is always death. And there is always rebirth. It's an endless Program.

The Centre

There are two Centres. The Tugh Centre, manifesting the body of the universe, and the Bhan Centre, manifesting the universal mind. The Tugh Centre right now dwells near the core of the Earth and has been there for 2.4 billion years. During the present Global Round, which began approximately 16,000 BC, the Tugh Centre has incarnated in human form sixty-two times. The Bhan Centre dwells in the heart of the Sun at the source of the string. In this Round, when not in its place at the Sun, it has incarnated eight times.

The Bhan had lost love and found form. Out of form it is dormant. In form, it builds. The Bhan Centre sits at the heart of Sun and filters the string. But it doesn't create the string. This is the job of the Dog. Just because the Centre is the source of our consciousness does not mean it creates what consciousness is as a whole. It's only the beginning of a vast process. While it's true that the Centre impacts everything down the Fractal Lines, consciousness as a whole exists only when each and every Crystal – and that includes you – does its job of filtering, of de-coding what it received from the Crystal in front of it on its Fractal Line. So it's all the Crystals together creating that ocean of information, of consciousness. It never stands still. The Dog producing neutrinos and all the other Crystals changing the stream all the time, down the Fractal Lines. Always receiving, changing and transmitting information. And that's why consciousness is an evolving thing. It's not an absolute. The only absolute is the filtering potential of our Crystals. That's why we call them Consciousness Crystals. It's a Program that is writing its own code, its own software over time. It's self-evolving. That's why we all are creators without choice. We are all influenced by an aspect of the whole. There is no *one* truth.

The Camel and the Dog

These two Crystals are housing the Centre between them, shrouding it. They are special Crystals because they live in the Sun and are responsible for our consciousness. Only the Camel and the Dog are first-generation Fractal to the Centre. The fact that there are three Crystals in the Sun leads to an understanding of all those various trinities that have been around for years in all kinds of belief systems: Brahma–Vishnu–Shiva, or Father–Son–Holy Ghost, and so on. I think it's fascinating and rather odd that, according to Christian mythology, it is written in the New Testament that for some reason dogs are not welcome in heaven. This should give some pause for thought. The Dog represents the fundamental programming of human consciousness. The Sun's Dog is our source of knowledge.

The Camel and the Dog each incarnate once a Round, approximately every 19,000 years, never in the form of humans or Raves. The Dog manifests and maintains the body and life of the Sun itself. It's the Dog that generates the neutrino stream. The Dog is actually maintaining the Sun itself. It has nothing to do with the rest of us. Its focus is only to maintain the power of the Sun, the fusion process that is its life process. The neutrino information that is coming out of the Dog is going to be filtered by the Centre, and out of that filtering is the actual programming source that is going to be there for the Solar System.

In this Round, the Dog has yet to incarnate. The Dog generates the neutrino string, so when it incarnates on Earth it can't produce the neutrino string from here. It means at the astrophysical level, there is a sputter in the fusion engine of the Sun.

It's a major trauma for Earth when this takes place. The physical body of the Sun is disturbed with vast increases in the output of ultra-violet energy waves. The Dog usually incarnates at the lowest levels of life, and never has been in form longer than three months. It will incarnate again in July 2084.

Perhaps the Dog will incarnate into a microbe with a life span of 18 seconds. The Voice didn't say.

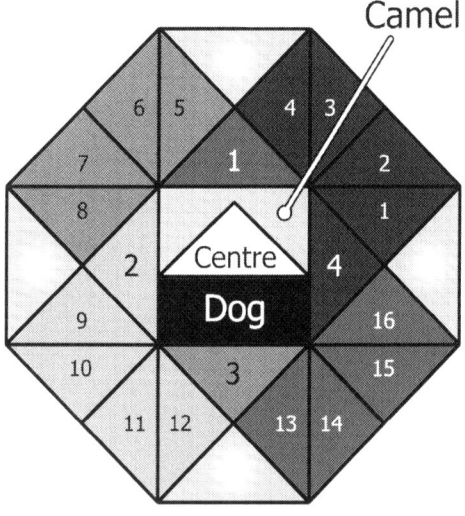

If it's going to be longer than 10 minutes, logic says this is going to have a very disturbing impact on the planet. However, it is something that has happened before. It just hasn't happened in the last 19,000 years, so who knows what it was in the past and what the consequences were. It's not something that happens often, and obviously it's an extraordinary marker. It also means there will be no information from the Sun the moment that the Dog incarnates. In other words, that solar programming for as long as the Dog incarnates is going to stop, which means that the only programming that will exist will be stellar programming and will be whatever neutrino programming is available from Jupiter. The lunar nodes are going to be the most significant activation when that takes place. We don't know what it's like to be in a world without the imprint, the programming of the Sun. After all it's 70 percent of our programming. And think about the children being born in that time that will not be imprinted by the Sun. We don't know what any of that means.

What the by-product of that is going to be is hard to say. For example, the Earth is already experiencing an enormous depletion in its ozone layer, something that is supposedly the by-product of the greenhouse effect and the by-product of the pollution in our environment. The ozone layer opening up is only a concern in the sense that it allows in ultra-violet light. The ultra-violet light that comes in is a sterilising and blinding agent. So this output of high ultra-violet light energy and the continued breakdown of the ozone layer may, in fact, also represent a great deal of life-force damage that could take place at this time. It's hard to be able to predict any of that, because Ra was given no explanation and simply told it will be a major trauma. This is something that will be a vast shake-up and ultimately will very much have to do with people's geometries.

What is clear is that this is a monumental event. These are the kinds of events that come in the closing of the Round. And I'm not talking about the closing of the cycle in 2027. I'm talking about the closing of the Round, approximately 1,000 years from now, when this whole experimentation of self-reflected consciousness in form is going to come to an end. I think this is all about that process of bringing these things to their culmination.

The Camel, like the Centre, also filters string. While the Centre and the Dog can be stationary, the Camel never stops moving. It's tracking something. Its rotation within the Sun is exactly synchronised to the motion of Mercury. Mythology says Mercury is the planet that most loves man. This is Prometheus, the great gift of the gods to humanity. What all this means is that the Centre can never directly inform Mercury. The Centre spreads its information out to the whole Solar System, except Mercury. Mercury has a very special place. The old mystic writings say it's considered to be the Sun's older brother. The filtration of the string by the Camel is experienced by Raves and humans as their Personality consciousness. So from the moment your Personality Crystal enters your body, the programming of the Camel through Mercury is specifically influencing and programming that Personality Crystal of yours. In fact, for the first 88 days, a human or Rave foetus will only respond to the programming of Mercury.

Once a Round, the Camel incarnates. It incarnated in 1936 and returned to the Sun in 1941. It was the only opportunity for the Centre to directly inform Mercury since before 16,101 BC. The Camel was no longer filtering the string for the benefit of Personality consciousness and you can see the instability and chaos that existed. It stopped a deep humanistic programming. We were reduced to being mammals. The veneer of civilisation was simply stripped away. It would take years after the return of the Camel for things to slowly heal. You also have to see that people born during that period received a very special kind of programming. Future generations from these people will probably produce the Rave children who will be born for the first time in 2027.

The Four Corners

The next generation Fractal after the Camel and the Dog are the Four Corners.

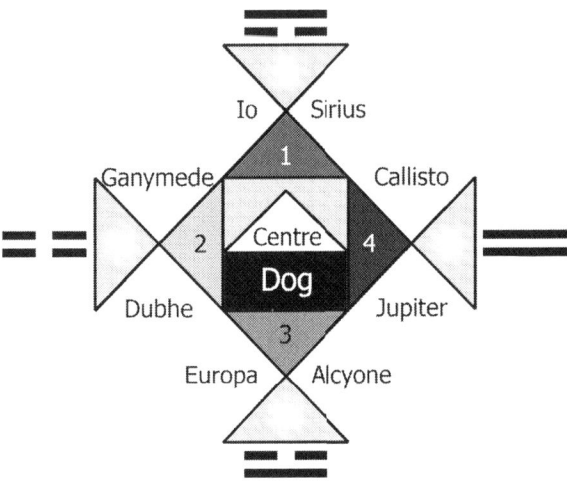

They sit in Jupiter, Sirius, Dubhe and Alcyone. Bhan Core Crystals (Personalities) usually only sit in stars and not planets, but Jupiter is a failed star and still produces a very low level of neutrinos. The Four Corners are directly involved in human and Rave Personality programming and establish the nature of the world. They manifest the archetype of the four and incarnate regularly. At least one is in a body once a century, sampling the environment itself as an on-going process of programming it. They can incarnate as anything – a microbe, an insect, a blade of grass, a swan, a goat and only sometimes as a human. To come as an animal protects them from being stuck on Earth for too long.

The orchestration of incarnation and the grand programming of consciousness in form is ruled by the Four Corners and especially Jupiter, the Logos. The King of the gods. This is as close as you can come to a description of the so-called monotheistic God. And this process is breaking down right now. We are coming to the end of the Round and it's already in the works, in fact since 1991.

The First Corner left Sirius and incarnated in Switzerland in 1991 into what would become a Yew tree. When this tree dies, life on Earth will end 1,300 years from now.

The Global Orchestration Directory (GOD) is falling apart, because one of the Corners is missing and not able to do its programming. It would be like somebody burning the Akashic Records. One of the things to understand about reincarnation is how complex it is. You've got to keep records, and it takes an enormous amount of organisation and resources to maintain the Global Orchestration Directories. The GODS, in that sense, are dying. The whole construct is beginning to fall apart. The ability to be able to maintain the reincarnative Program is beginning to collapse because the First Corner is no longer playing its part.

You can call the Four Corners "gods" if you will, but what you are really dealing with are very sophisticated Personality Crystals that live in stars and don't have the burden of living in a human body. It's just a mechanism. You don't have to glorify them as gods. They are mortal and not immortal. Sometimes their life spans are enormous, but they are mortal. Sirius is at the end of its rope. They die. Our star, the Sun will die, too. And the manager of this Round – the last 16,000 years – was Jupiter. All hail Zeus!

This Round has been determined by the reincarnative experiment. In other words, the constant testing of the same Personality Crystals through endless variations of vehicles to see whether the expression of consciousness in form is viable, and how viable it can be. It sounds like "somebody" is testing, but nobody is. It's what's happening. It was never about the Crystals (or the silly concept of your soul growing), it was always about the form, about perfecting the form. We are designed to now come to the end of this process. The Eron that will follow after will not have a reincarnative process anymore. When you look at the sky, you are looking at the past. Sirius is already gone, but we can't see it yet. It's Crystal is already in Switzerland. The Four has been reduced.

You have to grasp that there is a plug being pulled – it's all breaking down. The fact is that it's already over, but we don't know it yet. We haven't reached the point when it is obvious yet. But it has already happened. There is going to be a population crash as we move into the latter half of this century. It's connected to the fact that this Corner has broken down and it will have an impact on fertility and sterility.

If you look at the illustration, you can see that there are also the four moons of Jupiter: Io, Ganymede, Europa and Callisto. The three stars Sirius, Dubhe and Alcyone don't program us directly because we can't translate their frequency. It's Jupiter that translates from these stars to its moons via its extraordinary magnetic field. Within this field is all the stored information, what you could call mystically the Akashic records. Each moon is a microcosmic representative of the Four Corners.

But we don't receive any direct Personality Crystal programming from the Corners or the moons. They are operating at a deeper level, a chemical level, below the surface. You can see in this way that each of these Corners is impacting various areas within the Wheel, particularly their own zones (next chapters). If you look at the first illustration in this chapter, you see that every Corner/moon has a Hexagram couplet. You can divide a Hexagram into three couplets. So, for example, wherever you see a yin/yang couplet, you know this a chemistry that is impacted by Sirius/Io.

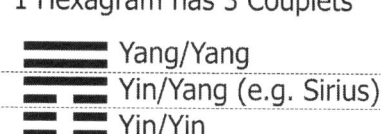

1 Hexagram has 3 Couplets
Yang/Yang
Yin/Yang (e.g. Sirius)
Yin/Yin

The Death of Sirius

If you go back to the beginnings of the great Egyptian civilisation to the first building of the first of the monuments – the way in which the architects and cosmologists worked in that era – you notice that everything was aligned to the star known as Draco, the Dragon. It was the brightest star in the sky. It's still a rather bright star today. But overnight, it all changed.

It was a deeply mystical event for those who were attuned to the experience. All of a sudden, out of nowhere, there was a new star in the sky. There were thousands of human beings, looking into a night sky, more black and full of light than any sky that most of us could imagine because we live in a world of so much artificial light. A new star in the sky brighter than all of the other stars was really something 6,000 years ago. It was magic. Out of nowhere, there it was.

If they had telescopes, they would have been able to see that star before it became a big shot because you couldn't see it with the naked eye. So what happened? What made it so bright all of a sudden?

Sirius was a singular star system that was passing along in a trajectory in which it was met by this dark object. Where the dark object came from, we do not know. Sirius attracted a dark companion – Sirius B. It doesn't give off any light of its own because it absorbs light. In other words, it's an object that's super dense. It has disproportionate gravitational pull, a gravity so strong that it can pull light into itself and turn it into matter. This rather inconsequential star suddenly became a binary.

The dark companion is a highly dense, or superdense collapsed star, probably a neutron star from some cataclysmic explosion earlier in time. It was travelling in space and captured by the gravitational field of Sirius. The first thing that companion did when it got pulled into the orbit of Sirius was suck the energy from Sirius, pulling the light, if you will, from Sirius into itself.

There are tribal groups in North Africa, they're called the Dogon, and they are fascinating. Part of their mythology is to not only worship Sirius, but they actually knew about this companion and have drawings of it. They were aware of the mechanics of that event. That's something rather extraordinary. Of course, this is a primitive culture, but they knew something. They had an extraordinary revelation.

Basically, what happened was that this smaller, denser object began to orbit around Sirius, and by doing so began to tear it apart. Not just tear it apart, but eat it up at the same time. In the moment that this dark companion was captured by Sirius' gravitational field, or vice versa, they simply met each other in the geometry. This was the moment that here on Earth – in relationship to its distance away, in our relative moment – we suddenly saw the emergence of this new incredibly bright star in the sky.

After that, everything in the Egyptian culture was aligned to Sirius, the Dog Star. The Dog Star became the main star of the sky. Abu Simbel, the ancient Egyptian monuments, the Sphinx – they all were aligned to Sirius. This was a big event.

All this focus was given to it, all this geometry, and temples were pointed at it. Isn't it interesting to think about the nature of that Personality Crystal sitting in Sirius and what it was experiencing throughout these thousands of years of being ripped apart?

Is Earth the planet of suffering because of Sirius? Is that suffering actually coming to an end now? It's just an interesting point. After all, one of the deepest programming themes that we have received – 25 percent if you want to look at it that way, of what we receive as a general organising principle – has come from a source that was slowly, violently being eaten to death. While this happened, it put out a neutrino stream of information. Now, it's not there anymore, and hasn't been there for a long time, at least in our terms. It's been gone since 1991.

Sirius contributed very much to the inherent value of violence on our planet. Look at the mythologies and Egypt to see what possible association are in all of that: these huge monuments to the vanity of being the most powerful. These monuments are war glorification monuments. They're nothing but descriptions of battles – rarely described honestly, mostly propaganda. This is Sirius. These huge, organised societies, enslaved in many ways to their gods. It brought control and all that goes with it, the moment that Sirius began to shine in a way that was unnatural. The greatest light in the sky is being eaten by its dark companion until at some point that light will go out. When the light goes out, this Round will be over. Life on Earth will end.

*

Each of the Four Corners are influencing us through a specific chemistry. But they are not the whole chemistry, they are aspects of the chemistry. So the impact that is taking place in terms of whatever is going on relative to Sirius can be seen in every one of our Hexagrams (Gates) in the way in which they operate. In other words: in the ongoing mutative process.

This violent devouring of Sirius by its companion brought us all this stuff: it brought what would become the state, the nation with its laws and institutions, with its governing principle of "top dog" and who is the "biggest star". The cult of the Personality. This is what Sirius brought us. This enormous infectious cult of the Personality. Ramesses – my God, what a joke this guy was! He gets to become pharaoh, which is already enough of a trip. You might as well just enjoy it, right? No, it's not enough. He's young. He wants to prove that he is top dog – Sirius. So, he goes off to fight the Hittites. They were the "bad tribe" on the block somewhere in what's now Southern Lebanon. He sets off across the desert with his army and he meets them in a place that still has all this violence, probably somewhere around Gaza. The Hittites butchered his army, and he's lucky that he got out of there alive. Maybe with a couple hundred of men, when he went in there with thousands.

Within 20 years – all over Lower Egypt – there were monuments to his extraordinary victory in this battle. This is Sirius. This is what Sirius brought us.

Now, that could seem like I'm painting a dark picture. But there is something we have to keep in mind about what is left of Sirius' energy. After all, we're going to continue to receive the remnants of that energy until the end of the Round. What Sirius is now, in its new life, has nothing to do with human beings, and has nothing to do with the way in which the totality is programmed in terms of our consciousness. That's over. We're dealing with the remnants of this death, because that's what it was: a slow dying. That carried with it a dark side, but what about the light? What did the light bring?

The light brought the ability to channel communal focus and energy into something that became enormously powerful, in the sense that it expanded the intelligence of the whole gene pool. The science that we enjoy today is no longer the by-product of an isolated genius sitting in his lab somewhere off in some castle. It's produced in scientific factories. There are millions of them, with millions of professional scientists. And it all began somewhere back in Egypt, together with the great bureaucracy that was also created there. This is Sirius.

The centre Crystal that resided in Sirius – that Crystal that took on its enormous role in our consciousness when the dark companion came – is not there anymore. And it's never going back. There will be no reincarnative cycle to follow after the end of this Round. Thirteen hundred years seems like a long time for a human, but in terms of the cosmos, death is almost imminent.

When you look at the sky, you're looking at the past. Slowly, but surely, the past will catch up to the future somewhere down the line. Sirius is not really there anymore. It's Crystal is in Switzerland. That star that had shone so brightly is dead.

What's out there are the remnants and the overwhelming last gasps, as the dark companion strips away the last of its life. It means we're not being programmed properly any more. The Four Corners have been reduced – there is something that has been taken away. It doesn't just go away, it is a deteriorating phenomenon. In other words, it is a slow process. By the way, at cosmic levels of time it's very fast. But in terms of our time? At the end of this Round, somebody is going to turn out that light. There is still light coming to us, there are still remnants of the information in the neutrino field pouring to us – the neutrino field that was released right up until 1991 – and we're still taking that information in. It's not like there is an instantaneous breakdown.

The Deterioration of the Yin/Yang

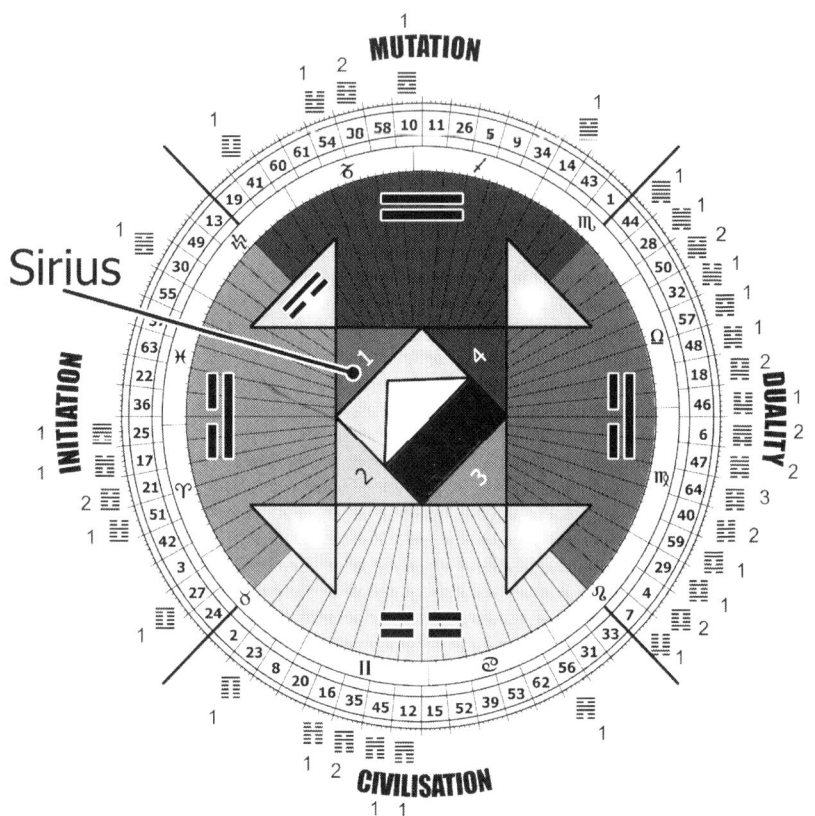

The impact of Sirius on the Hexagrams

Think about the places where the yin/yang couplet appears in all of the various Hexagrams – not just simply the Quarter that it is connected with. It's connected to what is its opposite in terms of looking at the Wheel, to the whole

Duality Quarter. This whole yin/yang connection is breaking down as well as the components that it represents. They are deteriorating throughout our chemistry and biology. It's the most fascinating thing. When you look at the configuration of the yin below and the yang above – this binary – we're not looking at trinaries any more. Instead, we see the basic triplets in the way a (DNA) codon or a Hexagram is structured – these three of two. We can see that this component is deteriorating so that the final construct can emerge. In other words, this is something that has to go, and what's really deteriorating the fastest is the top yang line.

In every single codon that carries this yin/yang as an ingredient is a deterioration taking place in the way in which it puts out information. Because everything that we see here is about dispensing information. The whole thing is an information system, all of it.

What Jupiter is doing with its tiny neutrino stream that it produces is that it takes in that information, translates it, steps it down in frequency, and puts it out as neutrino information that filters through its moons and to the 16 Faces and the Hexagrams.

Our time and what's coming is a "closing of doors". We are living in a period in our present cycle that we entered in 1961. It is going to end in 2027 by moving into a new theme. (page 149)

The moment we entered into this theme – if you look at it in terms of Global Cycle mapping, in terms of *locks* and *keys* – you will see this is a 61 era. In other words, "inner truth", both occult and exoteric, is only possible in this era, only now. This is the era of the *tree of knowledge* where all the fruit are available, but you still have to manage to get people to eat them. This door is going to close.

The age of innovation coming to an end – this closing of the investigative, collective, communal, cooperative investigation into the nature of being – all of this is coming to an end. The inspirations about all of this are coming to the end with it. And all because one Corner is no longer functioning properly.

As we move towards 2027: this is the time to "know". When the generation born in 2026 dies, we will have lost the last remnants of true inspiration that has guided our process. It'll simply be over. Revelation and those kinds of things will have come to an end. There will be no answers available if the answers have not been found or shared between now and 2027. This is really a closing of that door. Things are disappearing and will no longer be made available to human consciousness. We are in a great time of change. It's wonderful to be alive and aware, to recognise the mechanics of the universe, and to really see them at work.

It's just incredible to see this huge, vast, beautiful – so aesthetic – gorgeous organising of the whole process. To see clearly that reincarnation is coming to an end – if I can use that language – is a great victory for consciousness. Getting to this point is something that is important for us because it opens up the platform for receiving the Personality of the totality. It opens up the final stage of the development of the whole.

It was a long path of experimentation – the suffering of humanity, all the pain of going in-and-out and in-and-out, not knowing why – all of that to serve a greater purpose of the potential of a form that truly can house a consciousness that we ourselves are not even capable of glimpsing. If you follow the Program, it seems we're on track to fulfilling that potential. And all because the number one Corner is disappearing.

The mechanical process, the whole purpose of the universe, is to create the ideal form. A form that can nurture and filter consciousness to the point that the consciousness is self-reflected, that a *Maya* is generated and that the by-product is quite frankly "brilliance". No matter what my mundane views of humanity might be, my cosmic view is one of great delight. There is this spark in so many creatures. The purpose of life, the purpose of the universe, is the form principle. When you're building form principles, there are things that work at one stage and don't work at another. Whatever happened to the teletype machine, or the telex? There are forms that have served their purpose and then disappear.

The 16 Faces

In this illustration, you see how the information flows outward from the Centre. The four triangles without numbers on the outside – in between the 16 Faces – are the four moons of Jupiter, translating the Four Corners.

Every god and goddess that humanity has ever had can be found in one of the 16 Faces. The 16 Faces of God, the gods. It's curious to think about. Imagine we are calling something Divine but it's really just a Personality Crystal in inanimate form. It's

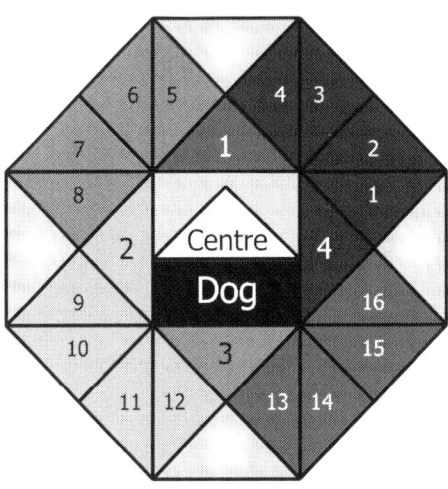

simply inanimate programming. They are not alive, not in the sense of life as we understand it. They are part of a life-force. And they are able to function out of the life of a star, which is a terminal thing after all.

The Earth is in a sheath of Personality Crystals. When you look at the 16 Faces, you are looking at the core infrastructure, with each Face acting in a sense like a Centre of the Crystal bundles that surround us. The Earth is sheathed in these Personality Crystal bundles. These bundles are absolutely enormous when it comes to numbers. The vast majority of these

Crystals in a bundle do not incarnate. Only sixteen, out of hundreds of thousands of bundles, are the source of most incarnating Crystals. Each Face acts as the identifiable Personality of the bundle as a whole.

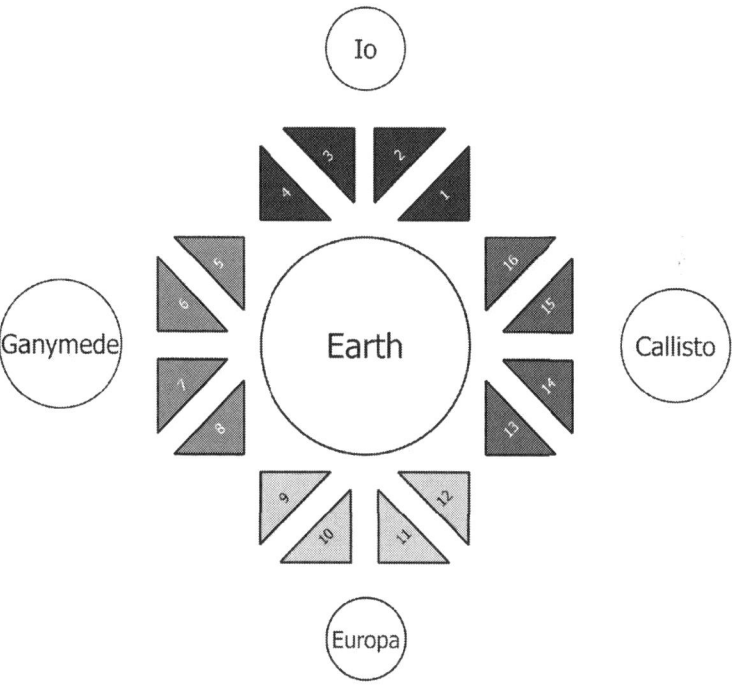

Each of these Faces has acquired a different value over time. They have been personal gods and goddesses. They have been the Buddha consciousness field, the Christ field, all of these different kinds of ways that people try to express what in fact is just mechanical reality. There is a filtering system going on that directly influences us.

Before the neutrino stream reaches Earth, it has to go through all those Crystal bundles. Not only do they filter the stream coming from the Sun, but also the stellar background field going back to the Four Corners.

We all originate from one of these 16 bundles. At the end of this Round – in 1,300 years – four of these bundles will be annihilated. They are the ones from the *Quarter of Mutation*: Hades, Prometheus, Vishnu and the Keepers of the Wheel. All the yang-yang Crystals. A mass culling of Personality Crystals has already happened before in time. This time they will be burnt in the centre of the Sun over a long period, which in turn will release their information as neutrinos. Nothing is ever lost. The Eron Mandala that is coming long after this Round will have only 12 Faces and no longer 16.

What we see here is four gods being turned into mortals. At the last incarnative sequence, at the end of this Round, the 1st, the 2nd, the 3rd and the 4th Face – all the gods that served Sirius – will incarnate into form as a plant, like Sirius already has. They will become mortal. Their power and influence will end and there will be no more incarnation. The genetic construct of life will break down. The Wheel is turning – but at some point it's going to collapse. It'll simply break down and dissolve, like the illusion that it is.

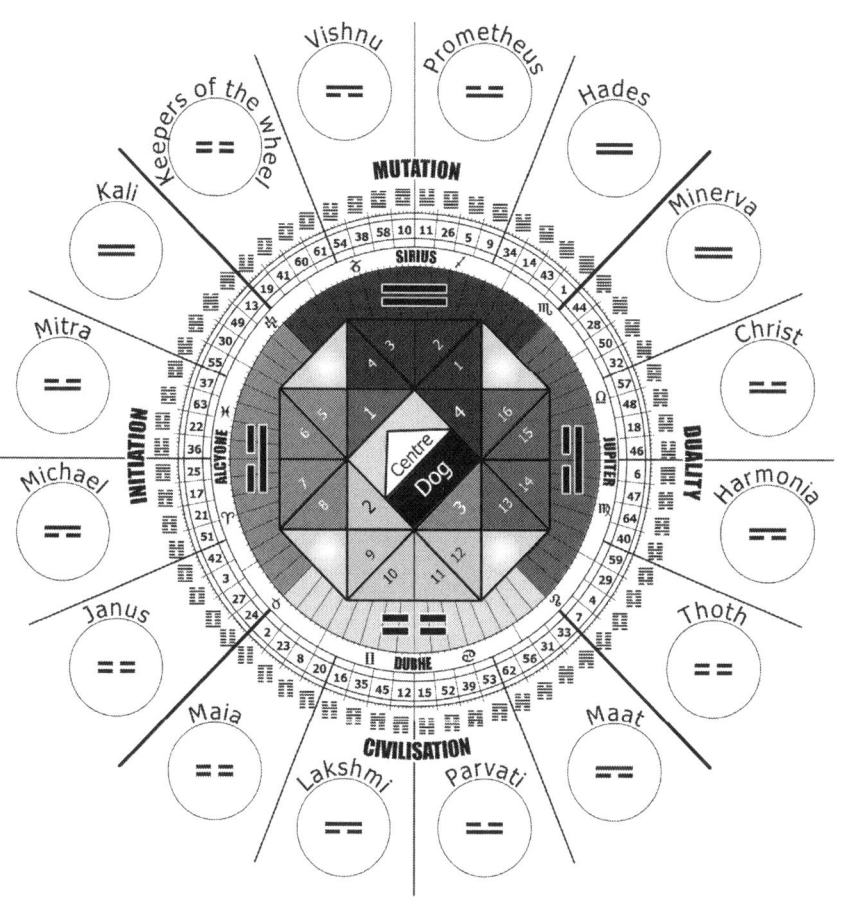

The 66 Sides

There are 66 stars, and we know their names, and they know ours.

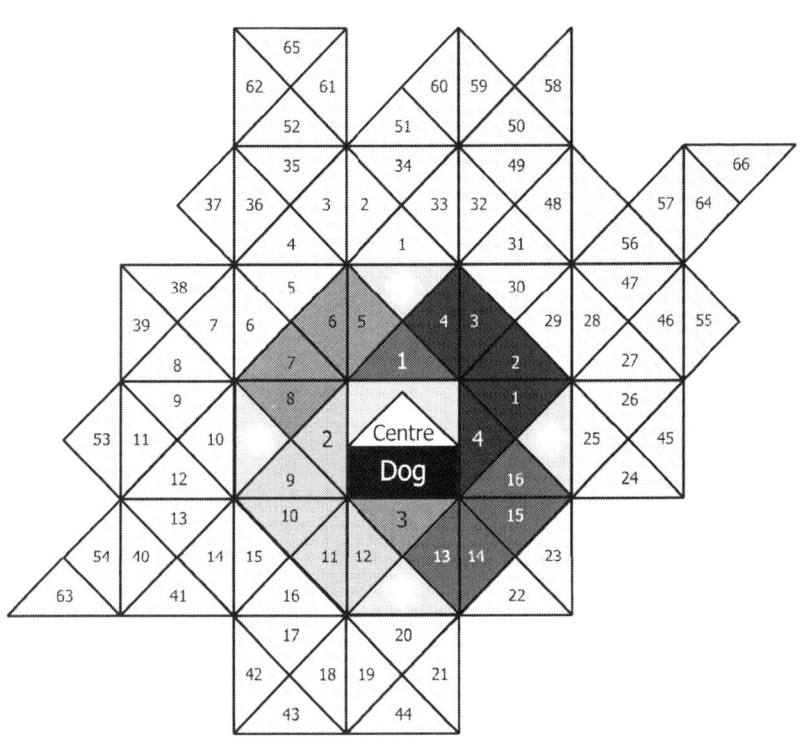

1	Difa	34	Arcturus
2	Pleiades	35	Ras Alhague
3	Hyades	36	Mulam: the Root
4	Aldebaran	37	Polis
5	Rigel	38	Mirach
6	Antares	39	Deneb Kaitos
7	Rastaban	40	Agena
8	Vega	41	Spiculum
9	Altair	42	Talitha
10	Fomalhaut	43	Almach
11	Deneb Adige	44	Rana
12	Bellatrix	45	Caput Algol
13	Capella	46	Alphard
14	El Nath	47	Al Jabhah
15	Polaris	48	Benetnash
16	The Pole Star	49	Caput Hercules
17	Betelgeuse	50	Alpheratz
18	Pisces	51	Algenib
19	Canopus	52	Phact
20	Castor	53	Alphecca
21	Pollux	54	Acubens
22	Procyon	55	Merak
23	Serpentis	56	Ras Elased Aust
24	Algenubi	57	Thuban
25	Regulus	58	Terebellum
26	Mizar	59	Albali
27	Denebola	60	Nashira
28	Markeb	61	Gienah
29	Algorab	62	Sadalsuud
30	Spica	63	Alnasi
31	Dheneb	64	Zuben Algenubi
32	Hamal	65	Kornephoros
33	Algedi	66	Achernar

Everyone is Magical – Each of Us is Unique

In the moment you truly embrace uniqueness, you are divine. It's so hard for human beings. We're caught in this vast generalisation and homogenisation. We're all lumped together, and yet each and every one of us in the potential of our uniqueness is absolutely, incredibly perfect, and dazzling in our perfection. There is nothing like you. Each aspect, unique in the shattering, creates the potential of uniqueness. You are an essential ingredient of the whole. It's not like you have a choice about whether you are going to be here or not. It's knowing how magnificent you are. We are all essential. But it's not like we really understand. Do you think that the cell operating somewhere in your frontal lobe knows what the hell your life experience is about?

It doesn't make any difference where you are in the hierarchy, where you are on the Fractal. We are all essential. So loving yourself is something that is profoundly magical. There is only one you. There is nothing like it. No comparison, no better, no worse, no *this* or *that*. How can you compare? Life will make sure that you are always in the right place with the right people. It doesn't matter if you are high or low in the Fractal. It doesn't matter if your outer life seems important or not. It's all about being where life needs you, and not where the vanity of your own mind thinks you should be.

Being alive is the expression of love. We are not loved. We *are* love. We are it. So you might as well stop looking for *it* because *it* is *you*.

Love Comes out of Deep Surrender

It's in this very deep surrender that you find your uniqueness, and in that you find your beauty. Every step of the way back to the beginning, our Crystals have been an integrated part of the whole.

Think about your Personality Crystal. Think about neutrinos going through it – programming and being programmed. The neutrino goes through. It leaves off its information, but it also takes on information. Your Personality Crystal has been programming the totality for as long as there has been a totality. It has been hard at work for 14 billion years and then you look at human beings on the mundane plane, and see how sorry they feel for themselves! How useless, inadequate, and undervalued they feel, all this stuff that we hear.

We are Building the Universe

If you look at all the Consciousness Crystals on this planet, they represent the potential of the brain of the totality. This is what it's all about. We are designing the nature of the vehicle, the Child. We are building the universe.

2027 and the Beyond

The Nine-Centred Transitional Form

Before 1781, humans had a seven-centred Program, the body of Buddha, the seven Hindu-Chakra body. There is no other species on Earth that has gone so rapidly through so many evolutionary changes. We are a deeply mutative creature. The seven Centres in the Graph were once five, and before that, there were three. The seven-centred being was a kind of "perfection", whereas the nine-centred being is a Design of "potential".

In 1781, Homo sapiens came to an end and now we are in a kind of interregnum. This is why it's so difficult, but it also offers us something that never existed:

If you look at all the religions, they belong to the seven-centred being. They don't really have a place in the nine-centred being anymore. We have all been conditioned by our seven-centred history. Think about morality, all those basic themes of right and wrong. They were all developed in a seven-centred, singular world, and all of sudden you get to 1781, when astronomer Sir Frederick William Herschel saw Uranus for the first time, which was the beginning of the death of the one God and this whole trip of finding oneness, a seven-centred trip.

Everything we have been and still are is the power of mind, but what's coming is the breaking away from it.

The Rave will be heavily influenced by Feeling Centre, and this will be everything for this being. We have to free ourselves from just being a poor copy of an extinct form that no longer exists. It's not about the mind anymore.

*

That transitional form has to serve two beings, two different species. It's incredible when you think about it. And it's always been like this in the past. We always had transitional forms so that out of the old the new could then emerge.

The Rave that comes in 2027 will be born out of our transitional form. All of this gives us enormous opportunities, but also places in front of us enormous barriers. The real human is already gone. Think about the last seven-centred baby who was born before 1781. It wasn't long ago – some of them might have lived to 90 years – that we still had them in the world. Every day that we get closer to 2027, there are changes taking place in the very form we operate in.

The mechanism largely responsible for that is Pluto. Pluto is different. It doesn't belong in the family of the planets. It's the instrument of the step-by-step mutative transition. With every step, it opens up the possibility of the Rave and diminishes the potential of the human. It is the great god of the underworld. It is a grace to embrace the power of a door-closer. It is what *Hu* in Ra Uru Hu means. The title that was given to him by the Voice. It means *door-closer*. That closing of the door can be so perfect, because as we move closer, things are revealed. Pluto is the instrument of this transformation from 1781 to 2027, of this new awareness based on feelings. It's waiting for its moment to shine.

We'll have 1,300 years with these two different beings together on this plane. You can't close the door until there is potential to get it all, to understand everything. It doesn't mean that everybody is going to get it. It never happens. There are always Fractals that get it, and some where the door slams in their face.

We're having this enormous population explosion that is necessary for the mutation to take place in 2027. This is not for the benefit of the individual human being. We also have global warming. All these things are needed. We are here to be of service to the evolution of consciousness – no choice. Autism and prostate cancer are by-products of the mutation taking place, all sacrificed for the transition.

When Rave children emerge, they will all have a priority based on *feeling*. The Rave will enter into a world that you and I can never know. Although we will be in the same place dimensionally speaking, we will be in totally different worlds.

When 2027 comes, there are two issues to deal with: first, our own possibilities and, secondly, to close the door correctly as our species. At the same time, it's our responsibility in an altruistic sacrifice to nurture the emergence of the Rave, those who are intended to replace us. When we will look back in 300 years to this epoch we are living in, we will see that it was really something special. It will be seen as the time when the door on humanity closed. It closed with the *Cross of the Sleeping Phoenix*. 1781 to 2027 is a very special time.

We are standing on the edge of something that is profound. The time of innovation is over, and it takes time for those beings born before 2006 to peter out. It's a slow process, but it's already under way. We are crossing lines in 2027, and we cannot go back to what was before. There is a beauty that is there for everyone now, but there could be also a lot of ugliness when the shattering takes place in that transition of cycles. There will be so many who will suffer as a result, and there will be those who will thrive. There is nothing else you can do.

Raves will have the same Graph as we have. But the Rave and the human will have their own "dimension" in the Graph. There will be different Circuits for each of us. The same Graph will be able to house different consciousnesses, alien to each other. It will be different to read the Design of a Rave. If we had enough time – and we don't, as we come to the end on this plane in 1,300 years – our kind would eventually die out. Then the final Graph of the one form after the transitional one would then emerge. The eleven-centred Rave.

The Rave is here to be part of a *shared* consciousness; a kind of cognitive process that is the completion of our evolutionary track.

Think how long it has taken our kind from being conditioned by all the forces to finally get to a place where we can stand on our own feet, on our own Authority? What a journey it is to leave ignorance behind and to find awareness, to come to our own differentiated and unique truth. The Rave does not have the same luxury that we humans had in terms of time. We had approximately 150,000 years to get to that point. The Rave only has 1,300. It will have a small population to begin with, peculiar circumstances that are going to limit the amount of potential they have to flourish, and on top of that they will have to learn how to operate as a melded consciousness.

We are dealing with an advanced form that will be primitive in its own relative development, and its deep dependency on the other, its own kind. How different from us! We are going out the door *alone*, but they are coming in to be *one in many*. And they will operate out of a different methodology for cognition.

Let's look at the human for a moment: we had a singular function and purpose, what we call in this context *strategic*. Everything about the success of humanity – the hundred thousand years that humanity operated through the seven-centred vehicle – was that it was able to establish through its strategic cognition its supremacy on the planet.

It's not surprising that many of us, since 1781, all of a sudden find discomfort in the treatment of animals as an example, or the conquering of *this* and *that*, or the rapaciousness of what seems to be the human appetite. In fact, it's natural for us now to do so. Although we are human and strategic, we also are in this transitional form that is deeply impacted by the emergence of *feeling*. It's not what it will be for the Rave, but it's there. It's an influence of how our variation of human works.

The seven-centred being was purely strategic. Everything was rooted in the themes of "success" and "figuring things out". Everything was about security, and everything was concerned about uncertainty.

Humans are visually acute, with the eyes so close together, so we can have depth perception of a calibre that is extraordinary in nature. It's all part of the strategic process. Humanity still operates out of strategic thinking as its homogenised way of understanding life. No matter where and in what society you look, you are going to see that the young are taught strategically. They are taught how to focus on problems, how to find solutions, how to protect themselves.

We have reached the end of human fertility with the *Cross of the Sleeping Phoenix* that is coming. Everything we understand as the reproductive process in humanity is going to be radically changed.

Basically, all technology we have today is still the remnant of the seven-centred world. There is no new technology coming that is going to transform everything. There is no "wonder-energy system" that is going to replace the depletion of the natural resources that we are using up. The boom is over. It's the serendipity of the car that is out of petrol and the station is down the hill. We humans are on that hill, just rolling down. We are out of juice. This is humanity. And the beauty – as there is always beauty – is that it can be consciously seen, and we can participate being a value to those *feeling* based children who are coming into the world.

For the human, the coordinating zone is the mind, and for the Rave, it's the memory. This is something very important for us to be aware of. The memory does not do the visual conceptualising that the mind does. It's a storage zone.

The Rave has no mind, but the moment the Raves are in a Penta, the Penta acts as the mind. It becomes this huge, complex, and extremely powerful entity. It does not emerge as a personal self-reflected consciousness. It emerges as a consciousness field, something that is very hard to grasp for us. A field with not just one member, but three to five of them, and the moment they are together, all of their depth that is in them is brought out through Penta activity. It's the Penta that becomes the life, and it is not a singular life.

When it comes to social evolution, humans don't do well. Ant colonies are the social epitome when it comes to social evolution. We humans don't know that. We have to use the internet and telephones. As a matter of fact, it is our purpose to fulfil our *separate* uniqueness. We are not Raves. You can see the vulnerability of the Rave, of this feeling-driven consciousness, that standing alone it is going to be handicapped.

When you will meet a Rave that is not in a Rave Penta, you will meet a handicapped creature who seems incapable of keeping itself alive, that needs to be cared for and that seems unable to grasp the simplest of the strategic. The only advantage for the Rave that is alone is the hope that it will be institutionalised. But the moment they get themselves a Penta in one of these institutions, the whole movie changes, because finally their mind exists and there is a conceptual facility for them.

If you are a human that is *feeling* driven, you have learned through conditioning to take advantage of the strategic mind, which of course leads to a lot of insecurity in the strategic thought, but nonetheless, you have been conditioned how to use it. But the Rave infants will not even be able to take in that conditioning. They live in a domain that we don't understand. It's not so much about sharing this Earth together because, in fact, in many ways we will not be aware of the other.

When you think about the strategy of the Rave Penta, one of the most interesting things is that it has no Success, no

Knowing, and no Feeling Centre. The Penta itself as an entity isn't reliant on these. It has its own inherent strategy, which is *material-plane dominance*. It's funny when you think about helping them, paving the way for them, but their consciousness is better equipped to dominate the world than ours. Ultimately, if there would be enough time, that's precisely what would have happened. Pentas are dynamically material entities. They are all about material direction, material development, and material display. This is the form mechanism at its very best. That Penta is much more powerful than its parts. It's incredibly sophisticated. Much more powerful than we could ever be.

One of the most significant mutations in human history was the mutation of the larynx. This mutation allowed the ability to articulate, expanding the potential for speech and therefore was the glory of the strategic human. It is clear that Raves are not going to be an articulating form. They will not need to be. Speech was valuable strategically. The ability to share information quickly and over distance gave human beings an advantage over their prey. To give sophisticated information was an enormous advantage for our ability to conquer the planet. So speech is very much part of the strategic. Raves are not going to have any interest in that, as there is no need to communicate because they are the Penta. We don't understand that, and it's difficult for us to grasp what that could possibly mean.

In the illustration we see the Autive Circuit of the Rave. There is no Channel 49–19. Those children who are born after the 15th of February 2027, no matter if they are Raves or humans, will all have a dysfunctional Channel 49–19. The Gates remain active as a potential only. For us humans, there will not be much of a difference, but the Rave will have completely new Circuitry, and yet, they have the same Channels and Gates. You can only marvel at the genius of the Design of this transitional form. The moment you separate the 19th from the 49^{th,} you bring changes that are extraordinary, for example, changes to our relationship with the animal kingdom.

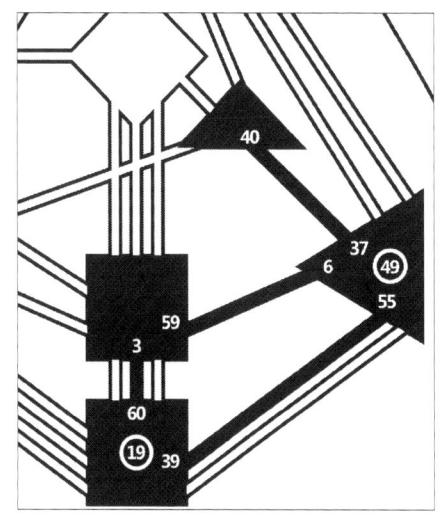

This is one of the bridges for humanity, our capacity to domesticate animals and be able to use domesticated animals to feed ourselves. I don't know what this will mean to domestic pets like dogs and cats, but it means they will no longer respond to the fact that we give them a controlled environment with food, and in return they do what we like. This is going to be different.

The 19th Gate is also the source for all religion and spirituality. It's all coming to an end, and this explains fundamentalism in all kinds of religions right now. They are all cranking up their game, because they can feel the wind blowing in their faces. It doesn't mean that it will all end in 2027. There are plenty of us born *before* who will carry it over the line, but it's going to end sooner or later. The 19th is also about the need for the tribe, the driving force for the tribe. It is going away. The underpinning of community will disappear. The spiritual communion of tribes, the glue, the same gods, it all begins to fade and break down. It's a profound transition that will deeply impact everything. We humans have to see that we are entering into a very individualistic time. And this is the time for the perfection of the human.

The Design of Raves

Something really unusual is about to take place. Something that is so rare in the evolutionary process, these moments of the shifting. We stand before the sudden emergence of a new mutation, a new variation on the larger theme of the species.

It's not like we've gone through that many times. There may have been six or seven different variations in what we would call our family tree as a species. Obviously, these have been extraordinary moments in that you had a form that functioned and fulfilled its purpose, and all of a sudden had to leave this plane because it was no longer supported or fertile, whatever it may be. You have a new form that emerges out of it, and through this, it suddenly comes to take its place.

The Autive Circuit

Keynote: Meld

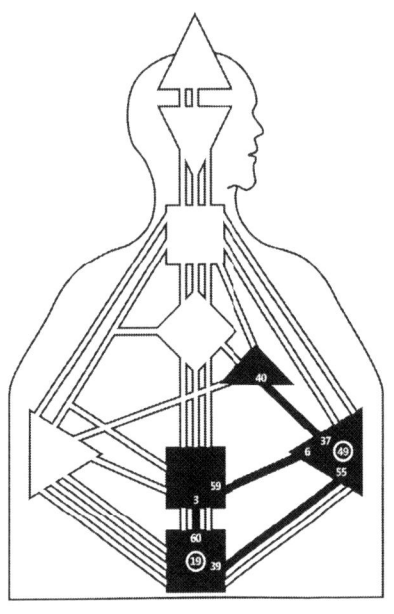

You have to grasp about the nature of the Rave that its power centre is here in this Autive Circuit. This is what it is all about. Not power in a way that we humans would understand it. We are dealing with the potential of awareness that is suddenly there. The Autive Circuit is nothing but a power configuration. The primary task of it is sending and receiving frequency, something we humans cannot really grasp. It has a keynote and it is *to meld*. It's a funny word that's not common, with not a lot of value to it. Melding is when unique things still manage to find a way to actually become one; a way in which they can connect at a level that is beyond what we understand on the surface and a mutual embrace that is seamless in a sense. It is leaving behind *unique differentiation*, and opening oneself up to *integration* into something that is holistically greater.

If you look at the middle of the Feeling Centre, you can see the 49th Gate, and in the middle of the Root is the 19th Gate. There is no Channel. The 19th Gate is not part of the Autive

Circuit. Therefore, you can't see it in the illustration. The 49th Gate assumes a completely different function the moment that we have the termination of this Channel, the elimination of the 19–49. We will see later the new quality in which the 19th Gate is going to operate also in humans born post-2027.

The Autive Circuit's Stream of Telling

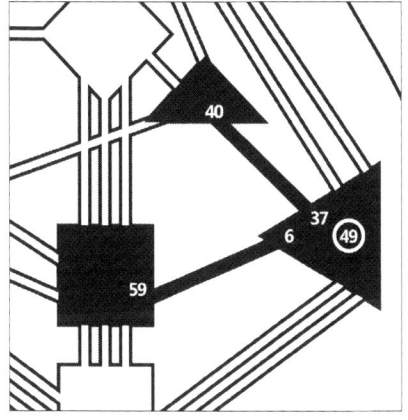

With a Circuit we are always looking at streams. When we look at the *Stream of Telling*, we see the capacity to share and to meld. This is the ability to bring frequency information and to release frequency information.

The Autive Circuit's Stream of Taking

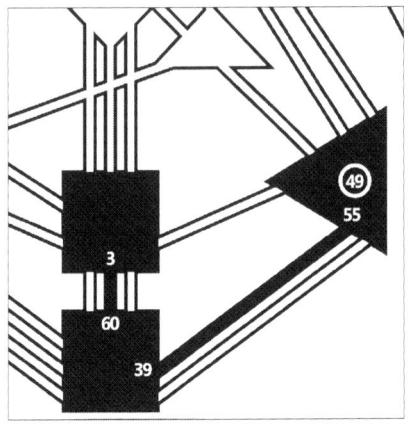

The second stream we see here is the *Stream of Taking*. So, we had one stream of *telling*, and now we have one of *taking*. This taking-in is fundamental. It's the awareness source for taking in. When you think of taking-in, it's more like breathing in for us.

The Gate of Access

We have two areas. We have a stream that is taking and we have a stream that is telling. And then we have something else. We have the *Gate of Access*, Gate 49. It is very significant. It is the coordinating point that brings together the power of the taking, with the capacity of the telling, in order for all of that to be able to emerge. We talked already about the fact that the Rave is going to be dependent on Penta and that it will operate through conscious Pentas, which is *melding* with the other Raves. It's different from a human Penta, which uses the Channels in the power column from the Service Centre through Love to Sharing. These Channels are not part of this Circuit.

The illustration below shows the Design of a Rave Penta. The Service Centre of a Rave is what hooks into the Alpha Lock of the Penta. This is the way the Penta is able to tap into this energy awareness resource zone. It empowers the Penta with self-reflected consciousness potential. It is much more profoundly aware than we are, and yet, strategically limited.

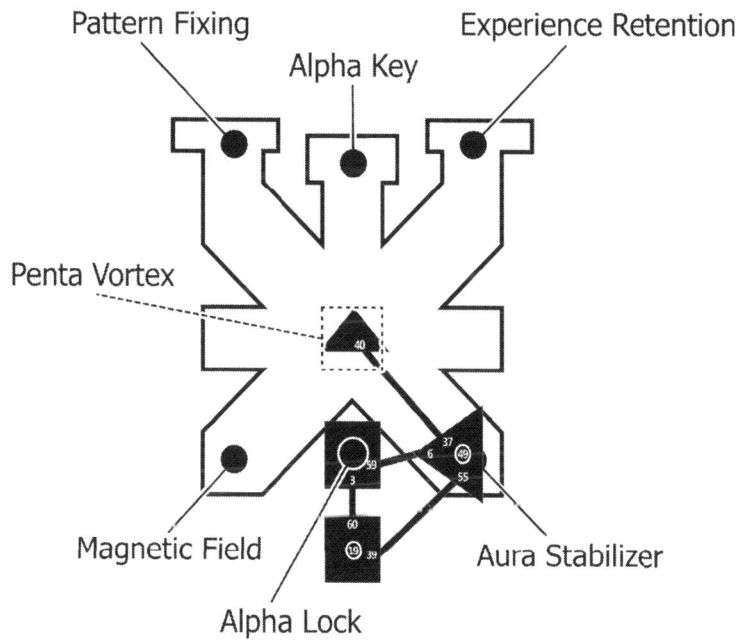

The Rave Penta will only have 12 Channels available out of which to operate strategically. This is much more limited than we as humans operate strategically.

Here, we see a special relationship between what we call the Desire Centre and the Vortex of the Penta, which is the central magnetic field of the Penta. Ultimately, it brings this potential of special willpower energy to the Penta. The Penta does not only operate as it does in humans with its materialistic direction, but this is a materialistic direction endowed with willpower. Here, we have the wilful expression of awareness, something that we humans don't have and don't understand.

The Channel 59–6 in context with the Rave is more a magnetic force that is pulling things into its Aura. All of this is to eventually have a survivable genetic pool, which means Penta upon Penta must be built up. The Rave is highly focused on attracting Auras.

Everything about the Autive Circuit has a relationship to food. The Rave is going to be extremely selective about food in terms of what is possible for the Autive to handle, and meat is not something that is going to operate well in them. The Rave will also no longer be pressured by the needs of the tribe, as there is no Communal Circuitry. They are not strategic. They operate out of an awareness that knows how to coordinate information. Because they have no emotional wave, they cannot be moody. That's why they will seem so flat to us. It's very different when a Channel operates out of awareness, instead of out of an emotional wave. Think of the moody Personality of humans that you can smell a mile away. That's no longer there.

Single Raves are absolutely helpless. However, a Rave Penta is anything but helpless in its capacity to take in all this information and codify it so it will be available for access from the melded consciousness. The only way that the Rave can survive beyond the charity and humanism of humanity is if they have a strategic capacity. They themselves individually have no such thing. But the awareness-endowed, wilful, and conscious Penta does. It's a *melded* awareness.

If the time ever comes that there are enough Raves, you will not communicate with one of them one on one. You might be able to communicate with the Penta and its awareness, but never with a single Rave. The Penta awareness is not the awareness of its contributor. If we look at this Autive Circuit from the broadest perspective, it means this is the instrument that makes conscious Penta possible.

The Experiential Circuit

Keynote: Collect

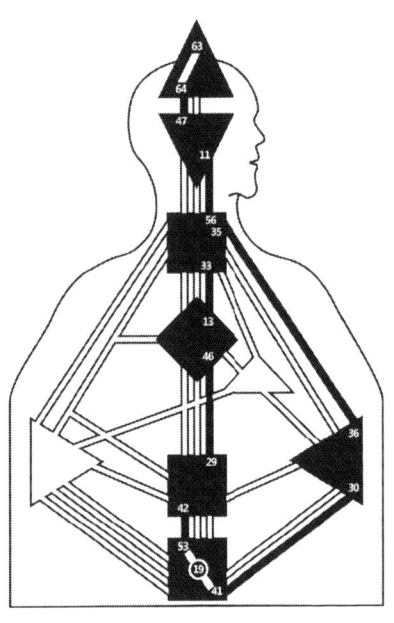

The Experiential Circuit is similar to the human Feeling Circuit, but there are fundamental differences, related to the 49th Gate, one of the implementers of the completion of the 2027 mutative process. The keynote is *to collect*. The *sharing* for the Rave can only be something that can be collected in the most extraordinary way. Even the infant Rave is absorbing information at a level that is thousands of times deeper than us and yet, we look at it as being so helpless and fragile. They are the great collectors, but not for themselves. They don't know *why* until they are a Penta. They don't try to make sense of the data they collect, but deconstruct and store it into its senseless bits so it can be reassembled. Their experiential plane is not connected to *achievement*, and they surrender to a larger force that taps in and will provide those things the individual does not have. None of us can imagine the impact it will have on us when we will first meet a conscious Penta. They will be anything but vulnerable, and never fear for their survival, because it's not their point. Fear is only something human.

The Collective Circuit

Keynote: Perfect

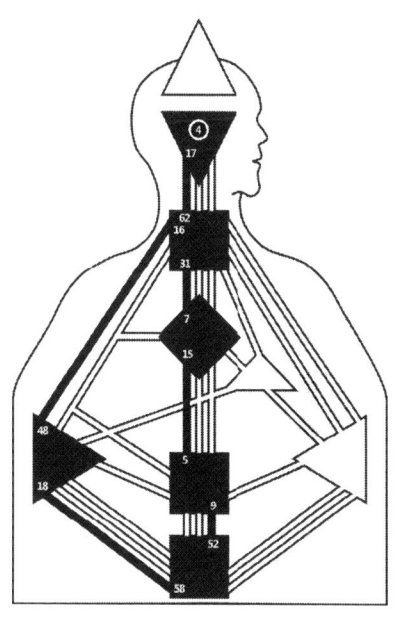

Right away, you can see that the Solving Centre is no longer part of what was the Success Circuit in humans. Success can never be enough, never be satisfied. Think about a pianist. They play a Bach concerto 2,000 times. Some people can be magnificent, but you can always be *better*. Now think about the Rave and what it means to be *feeling-based*. You can't be strategic at all. The Rave has no input in this Circuit. The Rave will have no fear, no doubts, and no God. These are all strategic values that were human. They won't develop new patterns with *Success* like we did. They only take everything in, and make it available to the Penta. It's not the job of the Rave to do something with the information. We can't understand that. Humans are fulfilled in discovering their own, unique path. Raves are fulfilled through releasing themselves to a transcendent consciousness. So different, and yet, out of the same box, out of the same form.

If you look at the evolutionary movement from Neanderthal to Rave, you see that physical strength and a heavy bone structure are no longer the point. The strategy of the Homo sapiens made it superior to the physically stronger Neanderthal. A small woman with a gun can rule. The form is devolving away from *strong and fast*. We come to bodies that don't seem to appear to do well on the physical plane.

If you look at the Circuits of the Rave, you can see how the Personality, is not invited in the process for survival. For example, the Solving Centre being cut off in the Collective Circuit. The Rave is no longer interested in itself as *itself*.

The Rave will never get the opportunity to live in its final 11-centred bio-form that will eventually come after this transitional nine-centred form we are in now. Raves are going to be limited in the nine-centred vehicle, in the same way as humans are limited. The development of the form principle is 3–5–7–9–11. If it weren't cut short, the new Round on Earth in 3,263 AD would have begun with the 11-centred form, of what the Rave ultimately was intended to be. Just as much as we cannot truly experience the seven-centred human any more, can the Rave, born in this interregnum, experience what might be or could be the full transition into its new species. It will be cut short. The Rave is never going to get the opportunity to live in that 11-centred bio-form. Life on Earth will be eliminated beforehand.

If we leave the Raves alone, other than helping them to get together, they will not go anywhere, because they won't have to. They will not live in the same world that we do, dimensionally speaking. Everything is about perception. That's what the

Maya is built on. You get up in the morning, you open your eyes, and this is the illusion you are accustomed to. The illusion works through the eyes, while once before it worked through the nose in our evolutionary story. Now, they are going to operate through *frequency*. When they do that, they are no longer seeing in a way a human sees. They will move from outer vision to inner vision, moving into a world that doesn't have trees, roads, or skies. They won't be there. There will only be frequencies. They are going to be interpreted by the Penta and shared by the Raves. We cannot know a world like this.

The fact is that we won't be living physically in the same world together. It is not that they will be taking away our Earth. They will have their own. An Earth we will never have access to, that we will never live in. A unique, dimensional environment based on *their* perception.

It's like watching a dog when it sniffs around a fire-hydrant. A fire-hydrant has been frequented by many creatures, and the dog busily sniffles away, which seems for a human quite a low act. And yet, we don't have a system that can't even modestly compare to that of a dog. What they take in as a smell is multidimensional and carries all kinds of information, far beyond anything we could have access to. It's another dimension. There might be four or five dogs going past this hydrant, doing their thing, and they can identify the species, the gender. They can pick up the trail where they came from, and where they are going to in terms of kilometres of distance. They "see" aromas. We don't see the world like our dogs do. The dog does not see us like we see them. The dog doesn't even hear in the same way that we do. Their hearing is so acute that we sound like bellowing fools most of the time to them.

The Rave will have its own world, this world of intense frequency. The one thing we should avoid is the illusion or fantasy that as humans somehow we will have this "special gift" of being able to interact with Raves. It's a vanity. There are possibilities, through understanding, to be accommodating for a species that you do not and cannot fully grasp. It will always be something that is alien to us, and not necessarily something that we are here to be attracted to. We are here to fulfil our own unique purpose, and by doing so, we complete our time and the purpose of our species.

Let the Raves deal with their purpose, which has nothing to do with us as human beings.

The Material Circuit

Keynote: Gather

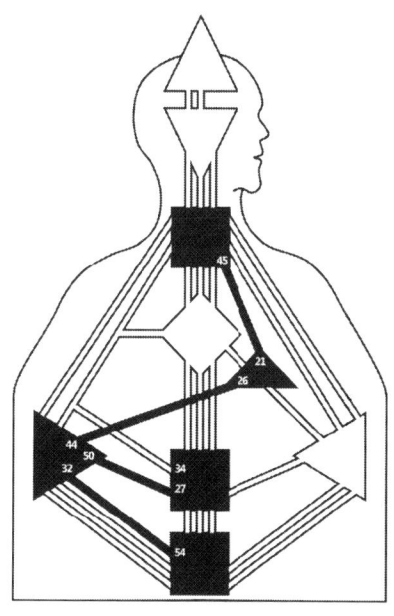

This Circuit really shows how much this being is dedicated to something that is not itself. From our point of view, the Rave is a "hard drive" attached to a Penta. We humans want to do something with the stuff we have, climb every mountain. It will be almost pathetic how Raves appear to us. The Penta is materially strategic, but it is not aware of itself. The Penta is not aware of its parts, and does not care how to feed them. But the parts are aware of *it*. It's not a form, it's a trans-auric form. It's just an energy field, a frequency field. This is where the consciousness is playing out. This is very sophisticated. It's much more sophisticated than us, where the consciousness plays out within the frame of the box, inside the construct of the brain, and only crudely gets out because we can speak.

We need to see how totally different all of this is. What we will truly have to deal with in the future are not the parts, the Rave, it is the quantum, the Penta; to recognise the Personality of the Penta, because that's what we have to deal with. That really is the mutation.

Compared to the Circuit in a human being, we notice that the part of the Community is missing here. Our approach to materialism is reflected to what we call in politics the left or the right. That is anything from capitalism to socialism, to give an example.

The Collective Success and Feeling have this sweet geometry on each side, with their own way to Sharing. But with the Communal, everything passes through Desire. There is no other place to go. The Community is about one thing only: *support*. That's what makes the Tribe human to us, because otherwise we wouldn't like it. We bring in this nice, social support. The social contract, the social bargain. The food, the shelter, the education. We are all a family. We have to look after each other and shall not forget the weak, the poor, the dumb, the lame or the blind. That's human, and you could almost say: "That's nice!" *Support* is different from *Collective Sharing or Inventing*. There is an intimacy and deep connection in order to *support* someone, to look after them and take care of them. It's built into us to be charitable, no matter how much money we make. It's called *support*. We are not so bad, it's our genes after all. We have a reasonable way to deal with the material plane.

Gather will not be like *support*. Have you ever seen a plague of locusts? The locust is very beautiful, but they are devastating, because they come in these vast clouds and literally eat everything. They are not growers. Humans learned that when you only gather you must be a nomad, you can't be anything else. Constantly moving, and through that, never being able to build a civilisation. So we developed the genius of gathering *and* restoring, so we can gather again. This Circuit of the Rave is not a grower. It does not plant a seed, it just gathers.

Everything about the Rave is to understand: it is not like us. The Rave is seeking homogenisation, but not in a way that we understand it, such as it leads us away from ourselves. Instead, it is a *melded consciousness* where the individual is no longer the point. If you isolate a Rave in a cage, it's dead, rotting, vegetable soup in a week. For the human to be alone is glory. The *I am*. That's us. That's not Rave. Rave is the anti *I am*. They're not into *support* in the way we understand it at all. The keynote *gather* is not about support. A Penta is a material strategic entity, and if you equip it with a consciousness pool, it is going to be good in gathering. Everything about its gathering is not about spending. Their intelligence has nothing to do with reproduction. They are not going to gather the way we gather. I don't expect them to be mobile. Their gathering will work in another way, and we will have to see in what way this will manifest. For most things, we humans can only speculate anyway when it comes to the Rave.

The human gave up most of its sensory depth for the power of the eyes. We are such visual beings. The power of the eye will be deeply diminished in the Rave, but oh boy, will they have something else! We ourselves are beginning to notice these frequencies that have been there since 1781; for example the whole paranormal investigation going back to the beginning of the 19th Century.

One part of the Rave is to take in the frequency information of any living or inanimate thing. On another level it's to make physical contact, probe anything it has contact with. In fact, they may be able to manipulate anything they can physically touch. The key is the frequency capacity, all those frequencies that being human is not really about and that we have no real access to. You have to grasp what that means: the moment you put these creatures together in a pack, in a Penta, something happens that is a level of quantum that is astonishing.

The Penta will be able to defend itself by being intrusive with its frequency capacity. It will be interesting to see how this will feel to us and what it can do.

The components of the Penta are these innocent receptive gatherers. And all of them, without doubt, without question or reason, or judgement, leave open the portals of their intelligence collection, and it is the Penta, as a melded consciousness, that takes all of that and uses it. There is a strategic disadvantage of the Rave as long as it's not in a Penta. But as soon as it is, we have a strategic disadvantage. After all, if they are going to survive in a world that is dominated by humans, they need to be really good. They need to be able to provide for themselves strategically.

What's interesting is to speculate how they will do that. Can one member of the Penta put its hand on a computer and through the Penta actually transmit information or even operate it? We are talking about sensitivity to frequency and information gathering. They don't have to know how to use it. They are innocent, sweet, little Buddhas. They wouldn't hurt a fly. Everything is "I breathe in for you", and the *you* is an *it*.

And the *it* is a Penta. It is the *it* that is going to tap into things.

It will display a strategic capacity that is going to make us humans look like Neanderthals. Trudging along with our huge club, hoping for something that is stupider than we are, so we can kill it.

The Rave Penta will live in a world of its own. It has no interest in being in our world. We are chaotic from their point of view.

They are going to take in so much frequency information that they will want to have some kind of Aura-clearance from humans, so they are not constantly absorbing all of that information that gets blasted out from the human domain. It can be assumed that their frequency range will be in kilometres.

The very first Penta that emerges will probably seek out the most isolated place possible within practical accomplishment. It doesn't need to integrate in the world the way we do. As already mentioned, it isn't going to eat the way we do. It will have a different diet and process its energy differently. So many things will be different about the Rave. I'm sure the Penta will find a way to deal with us, and there might be a person within the Penta who will communicate with us. Within the context of the Penta, they may be the best spokesperson, but it will always be the Penta speaking through them.

What we will see with the advent of the Rave is that it's no longer *form* that is the most important thing in order to create a state of consciousness. It's about the cognition of that *Penta*.

It's the Penta that's the evolution, the conscious Penta tapping into these resources and living as an entity that has no form, no body.

When we get to the logical conclusion of the evolutionary Program of cognition, we ultimately have to get to a vehicle that is solid, has no moving parts, and therefore is not in any way something that distorts the process of consciousness. You don't have to feed it, keep it healthy, or any of those things that go with it. That's our trajectory.

We are moving away from the form-experience in the world to the consciousness experience beyond the world. That's the potential of the Rave: to be a component of a consciousness experience that is beyond the form, and not interested in the needs and demands of the form other than to maintain the strategic capacity of that particular Penta.

Whatever is in their environment, they will take it in. Who knows? They may be able to take in nutrients in that way. Ra was never told anything in that sense about their eating process, other than that meat could not and would not be a part of it. How is that mutated stomach going to operate? We will have to wait to find out. How they will be nurtured? We don't know, but they will be. The material capacity of the Penta will guarantee it.

The Binary Circuit

Keynote: Caring

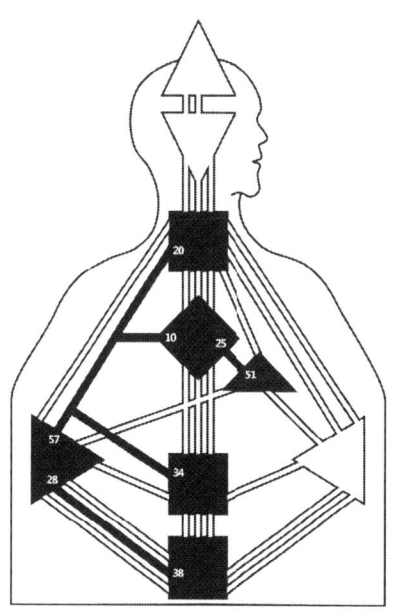

The Binary Circuit shows you how different the Rave really is and helps us to understand the difference between human and Raves. The Self-survival Channels in humans always represent the lone wolf and are the backbone of the individual survival process. But now you also have this strong desire in form of the 25–51. So here, all of a sudden, we bring processes together from three Circuits of the human. This sort of *caring* is different than what you would understand from a human. When we move to the age of the Channel of 20–34 in 2027, the *Cross of the Sleeping Phoenix*, what seems to us like the age of individualism is for the Rave an age of anti-individualism. It's this circuit that will strip the Rave from any individuality.

If a couple has one of these Rave children, they'll probably panic and feel all the sad things that go with this, because they'll think they have an abnormal, dysfunctional child. They'll be thinking what to do, the burden of it, the expense of it and so on. We already know that the individual Rave will be severely handicapped from our perception, and its motor processes and muscular development will be slow, because the Rave will be the first true Uranian creature. They will mature physically much slower than us. One can also assume they will have a different metabolism from us. What is so interesting about this particular Circuit is that it ends individualism.

Let's assume you have two Rave babies that happen to be in the same institution. They will immediately recognise each other, and although there is no Penta, there will be something. There will be what this Circuit brings. The moment one knows that there are two, they suddenly have been given the power to survive until there are three. Once there are two of them, they begin this process of *coming alive*. They are not here to be *one*. They are not here to be *two* either, but that obviously is a stepping stone. Even finding one in the beginning, when there aren't many, will be an incredible relief. They begin as a binary, and not as a singularity like us.

What is our responsibility in all of this? Will humans resist fighting a superior strategic force, even though it's basically an endangered species in its numbers? There are so many possibilities that it's hard to judge. It's hard to imagine when we leave behind the *Cross of Planning* Cycle how it will be in the homogenised world that lacks awareness. How many Rave babies will die in isolation? How many Rave binaries will hold on to each other in the emptiness of "no tomorrow" until there is finally a viable Penta? One thing is for sure: when there is that viable Penta, it will not need any help whatsoever.

The Individualistic Circuit

Keynote: Demonstrate

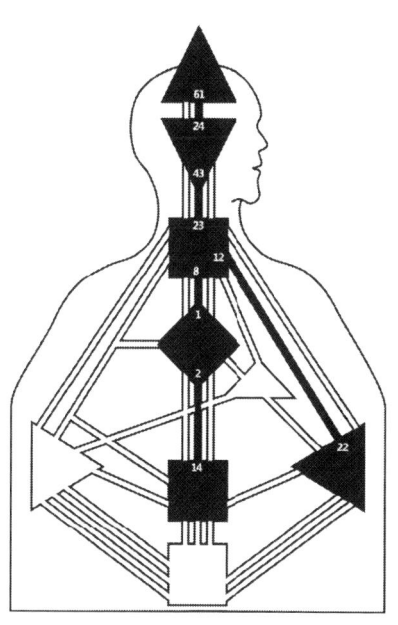

There are some interesting things in this Individualistic Circuit as it's stripped of its "Success dimension". It makes it different from what is its human equivalent. The most fundamental difference is that there is no *mutation*, which is what the Creative Circuit in humans is all about. There is no 3–60, so there can't be mutation. It's common for composers to come out of the melancholy, write brilliant pieces of music, and then go back into their melancholy. This Circuit is different. There is no *Stream of Emoting* as we know it in the human context. This is not a *mutative* Circuit anymore. No moodiness, no creativity.

It's really interesting to see how evolution operates. 100,000 years ago the mutation of the larynx took place. This mutation opened up the potential for the conceptual mind to relate and store the information of experience in a way like never before. The larynx dropped and it opened up the potential of the visual cortex, but most of all, it opened up the potential for a sophisticated nuancing of sounds in what we interpret as language. That mutation was at the very basis of the mutation of the seven-centred being.

This is what really separated us from our primate relatives. The only thing that was really similar between us and them is what we are like in the first year of our lives. At that age, we are able to do something that primates can do during their life-time. It is breathing and drinking at the same time. We see this in a nursing infant. While it's taking in the milk, it is also breathing through its nose. As a matter of fact, if it has a cold, it's a horror for it. And suddenly, when it begins to mature, as it's ready to be weaned, it starts having difficulty breathing and drinking at the same time, starts building up gas, and starts spitting back the liquid. It's the mutation taking hold. We cannot drink and breathe at the same time as humans, but it gives us the opportunity to express the complexity of the nuance of sound. The infant at that point has a limited acoustic vocabulary, the same limitation as the chimpanzee. It has always been clear that the Rave does not depend on articulation for expression. And here, in this Circuit, you can see it. This is stagnation. You could also call it the "stagnant Circuit". It's cutting off the individualistic direction. For the Rave, individuality is primitive. It's our glory as humans. And then you look at the Rave in this Circuit, and it says: "Excuse me? This is so primitive! This is so yesterday!" Any demonstration of individuality would be impossible for them.

Ra's assumption is that you will be able to identify a Rave when it gets to the age of between nine months and a year. You will notice that it will continue to breathe and drink at the same time. If the dropping of the larynx mutation does not take hold in that infant, we will know for certain it is going to be a Rave. If you are human, you will start to spit up after a certain time, and if you are a Rave, you will not.

The Rave will probably not even be able to understand language as we do. It is going to sound more like noise to them. The tone and frequency will carry more information than any of the sound bites for them. We are dealing with something that will appear extremely vulnerable and ill to us, but in reality it will be neither. There is a lot of possibility in this knowledge today, to give hope and courage to those parents who will get a Rave and probably be completely distraught, because they don't know what they are dealing with. It may not be always so, but nine times out of ten when a baby has limited acoustic capability and still can drink and breathe at the same time, well past the age of one, chances are that this one is a Rave. And it needs to be brought together with other Raves.

This Circuit shows that so clearly. There is no *mutation* left. It is stagnant. The only thing left in the 12–22 is its social quality. But there is a total lack of selfhood. The Love Centre will only become identity as it is expressed through the Penta. Raves are completely "flat". This is a locked flat and stagnant wave. They won't have any emotional wave like we had, because the Feeling Centre works differently.

If you look at sexuality, there is no Tantra, no sexual magic, or romance. It's doubtful whether Raves will experience romantic attraction. Something like that doesn't seem possible in a creature that has no selfhood. Mutation and reproduction will be stripped away from individuality and be placed into the Autive Circuit. There is no need to express oneself. There is no mind as we understand it, there is only storage. It's quite something to see this transition, but what it really means is that we humans no longer have the magic that is connected to our own process. It is connected in the larger sense to mutation of the Rave. This really sings our death now. It tells us that all of this, all of us, is primitive. There once were Cro-Magnons competing with each other, and there were Neanderthals in their non-competitive and communal frameworks. They were eaten alive. Their time was over. They lost their direction and mutative capacity. They began to lose their fertility and died out. It's a turning of the Wheel, and it's beautiful to see. This time we really get to see it consciously. To see the Rave, what they reject, and what they leave behind. Us.

Humans always have killed any kind of threatening consciousness in the past. Anything too smart or too challenging was eliminated. This has been the way for humanity to get to the top of the gene pool, by demonstrating it is the most sophisticated and capable creature on the planet. Everything it tolerates, it only tolerates because it is cute. The Rave is absolutely helpless as long as it is in isolation, to the point of being unable to survive. But if you bring three of them together, or even two of them as then their combined Aura will pull in a third, all of a sudden it's a different story.

*

There are always two sides to everything. We live in a duality after all. One side says: "Isn't this wonderful? Isn't this incredible? Shit, yeah, we are dying, but what the hell – there is something new coming! Can't we demonstrate how incredible, sophisticated, altruistic and wonderful we are, and provide for the Rave?" But then there is the other side. The moment you bring Raves together, you don't have anything that's helpless at all. As a matter of fact, considering that they may be very young, they may be quite unstable in how they use the power that they have as a Penta. You have to understand that a Penta will defend itself, it will look after itself. It is a strategic entity. The Penta will have an enormous database that is available to it. The life-force in any creature is always incredible. No creature simply surrenders itself to death, no matter the circumstances, regardless of its age or wisdom. And neither will the conscious Penta. So there is this other side of the story. It will probably embrace it with ease, and I doubt that in that moment humanity will grasp what the Rave really is. Fortunately, with humanity being a spectrum, there will always be those that do so.

It is necessary to see the mutation that will take place, despite of all this beauty, with realistic eyes. It may engender a lot of things that are not pleasant on all sides. There will be little reward for any human being that helps create a conscious Penta, other than whatever their own reward shall be. You will not get any reward back from the Raves. As a matter of fact, you will lose them as individuals. The Rave child of any couple – in its helplessness, which is still a being with a name, a focus of love and pain – once placed in a Penta, you will cut it off completely from the human world. It will enter into its own world from which it will never return from. We cannot know what we humans will look like in their world. They'll see us in a way we can't imagine. This will be quite a radical way in which the environment will be experienced.

In the same way as Cro-Magnon had binocular vision, Neanderthal had a weak visual cortex, and most likely saw in black and white with only motion vision. It's the same way with most dogs and cats, as they don't really see things when they are still.

Raves will probably not even see us in the way we see each other. It's unfair to compare. Even when looking at your dog, the way that dogs see us from their world, there are many criteria that we as humans would fail. It's never a question of feeling superior. We are just naïve in the way we project, even in the way we think our dog sees us. You can't project on the Rave that it is going to see our world, you and me, the buildings, the computer images. It has another world. It's a world that takes on a sense of purpose the moment they become a Penta. The Penta will accomplish its purpose by using forces we don't use and don't even recognise. This isn't anything like us. It's the same way as you might love having cats and dogs in your life, yet there is no way you can ever experience their world. We all have our own dimensions.

The isolated Rave is like humans in Eden. They had to be thrown out into the world. As long as the Rave is isolated, the process has not begun. Only when they begin the Penta process can they establish themselves in their world. They arrive in our world out of our wombs, and they step through the keyhole – the moment there is a Penta – into another dimension we will never have access to.

The Raves are the great collectors. Even when we look at them being helpless babies, they collect thousands of times more information than we do. Collecting, but not for themselves. Not knowing why they are collecting until they become a Penta. Then they will grasp what their solitary purpose is.

When we humans form Pentas, we constantly morph into Pentas and leave them, but once a Rave establishes a Penta, they will not break it again. Once it is established, it is going to be exceedingly difficult, probably impossible, to break out of it.

Let's say four Raves are brought together in a clinic, and someone wants to do individual medical checks on them. I can almost guarantee you that this will not happen. I don't think it is possible for a human or anything else to break the bond of a Penta once it is established. They are building a permanent formal entity, and they will stay that way.

The other question is: how are they going to reproduce, if they do at all? Will Pentas merge with Pentas?

They have a Penta that has no sexuality. A process of melding into one. There is no gender. Obviously, if the Rave would eventually flourish into an 11-centred form they need to be capable of procreating and reproducing. Do they need another Penta? Can a functional Rave Penta clone itself and make more? Does it even care? Will the conscious Penta in a nine-centred form even bother? Will it even be possible? I doubt that we can even catch a glimpse of their world after we bring them together to form a Penta. We have no access to their world. All we can see is just the wonder that it can happen at all, and we can watch it.

The Conscious Rave Penta

We are dealing with a mutation where the "strategic experiment" will be left behind. The *strategic* is human and only human. The mutation will shut down certain physical areas of the body and transform that energy resource, the saving, into a capacity to handle the environment, without having to do so on the physical plane. The Rave is going to look much worse than an autistic child. They will have a vehicle that is Uranian. As humans we cannot really play at the new physical cycle. We are all still attached to the Saturnian cycle. We have developed, through our self-reflected consciousness, ways in which we can enhance the potential of our vehicles to live longer to take advantage of it. The Rave is equipped in a totally different way. It no longer needs the brute, basic equipment. We have this movement that's taking place inside the Graph, as the last of the last, which is *us*, opening up the doorway to a new beginning, which is *them*. And how different this is. Their way of being able to handle the environment is far more sophisticated than our own. We have a curse, and it's *individualism*.

There is this story of the blind men and the elephant. One holds the elephant's nose and says it's a snake. The other touches its leg and says it's a tree. The Penta is *the elephant*. What does that say about the trunk and the leg? Can we think that way? Can we understand something that is alive, that has in a sense no purpose and no function? No capacity to do anything? If it is not assisted it will die, and yet, think what it is for.

The tendency is to think about *them* as you think about a human being, but you can't. In fact, *they* are not anything. They are the trunk or the leg, but that's not the story. It's the *elephant* that you have to watch out for. It is really something. How can a human being grasp that? If we think of a being like that, we think of someone who is a vegetable but, in fact, it's *the elephant*, the Penta, we have to deal with. Think about them when they come into the world, these "packages of meat", because *this* is how they will appear. Think about what happens when you bring three of them together and they become an *elephant* that has powers that are scary.

You can't explore the conscious Penta by exploring the Design of a Rave. *It* becomes conscious, not they. They participate in the process. It's almost like watching your mind. They will all watch their mind, but there is no mind. There is only application of resources. And believe me, Pentas will be good at that.

We are moving towards an extraordinary event at the end of this Round. We are about to enter into the full potential of the life of the totality. What will happen is that the universe as a whole will receive its *single* Personality. All of this, what we are going through, is preparation for the consciousness of the totality. Everything about the Rave and evolution is about how to surrender to a single Personality, the perfecting of the pathway to surrender to a single Personality. What we will see in the next chapters of this book, Brahma's Night and the Eron (the form that is coming long after life on Earth has ended) is that this vast universe will be endowed with a single Personality.

We're reaching the end of something. We're reaching the end

of selfishness in a sense. We are at the end of a story that says "You alone must get there!" It develops all the infrastructure for the evolutionary movement forward. We are soon to become yesterday's creature. The Rave will look like us when it comes out of us, but they will be not like us at all, and we need to be aware of that.

This stage in evolution is here to show that the potential of Personality can be housed in form. This is the story that is at the root of the beginning, the Big Bang; the Bhan and the Tugh that are, in fact, two Design Crystals.

There is no real Personality yet. Our Personality Crystals are "stand-ins" for the possibility of the real Personality.

Each of us is an experiment whether unique Personality can truly be demonstrated.

That's why it is a goal for us as humans. Since we entered into the nine-centred being, it was evident that the Personality could function in form, and now evolution will take the next step: can the Personality be the focus of *many* forms? And therefore you get a deeper and more powerful force. The stage that this is played on is vast, and at the same time it's small when you look at the stage of the totality. This is where we are going. We are going into a future where the perfected uniqueness of different forms together house consciousness. The perfect form for the ultimate self-consciousness principle.

The *universe* as consciousness. It's quite a thing. At the moment we are sitting in the dark, wondering: "Where is the light for the totality?" It comes at the end of this deep, inner movie, it comes with the birth of the universe in over two billion years.

The Penta will have access to information that is startling compared to how *we* process it. Do not think for a moment that these infants, once bonded into a Penta, will lack anything. Their world doesn't have the same kind of boundaries that ours does. You can hide behind a door and nobody sees you, but the Penta can see you. It won't "see" you, but it will know you are there. Not only will it know you are there, but know your heart rate, know what kind of chemistry you are giving off – a lot of things – and it will not interpret them as our mind interpret things. Therein lies the spookiness.

How did Neanderthal die? Did Cro-Magnons kill them off? We don't know. Did they look at them as we look at monkeys? They had no Desire. Not being strategic, their lifestyle would have been enormously different. It would have been similar to any kind of grazing mammal, passive in their relationship to their world. Or was it their time? Their fertility decreased and they died out? Or was it a combination of everything? It is clear that fertility of humanity will be less and less, but it is also clear that humanity will still be here to the end of the Round in 1,300 years. It isn't designed to perish in a hurry. Neanderthal and Cro-Magnons lived together for possibly 20,000 years often in the same places, like modern-day Spain. Will there be a "witch hunt" when humans see the first Penta emerge? We can't know. No matter how much we talk about it, not one of us can imagine how startling it will be to eventually meet it: this "thing", and its Personality.

*

Pentas always want to be with similar Pentas. You can see that with humans in cultural groups and language groups in cities and areas. This is what Penta loves. Rave Penta is going to look for other Rave Pentas. And when you bring together 81 Rave children that's the only time they could actually eliminate humanity. Ra had speculated that we will never see 81 Raves together as long as there is an Earth, but truly, who knows? Eighty-one is a magic number. It is the basis for the viability of a long-term gene pool. The moment you establish that gene pool, it can grow and dominate its environment.

If we were to have another Round – and there were many Rounds before, not just one – the Rave would be an 11-centred being. The nine-centred form is only an interregnum. We left behind the seven, but the goal is to get to the 11. To get there you need this basic structure, what can work from *this side* and from *that side*. The *bridge*. For the Rave it will never be a question of obedience or "Should I be part of this Penta?" They are not human. There is no "strategic". There is no individual. They are perfect collectors, whose perfection leads to incredibly powerful demonstration of the Penta. If you bring 81 of these together, they will control everything, and they will push everything out of their way.

The comparison between a functioning Rave Penta and a human being is no comparison at all. I try to keep a positive perspective of what a Rave is and how humanity could or would deal with it, but you also have to be practical and have no veil in front of your eyes when it comes to the nature of humans.

Humanity had to live out the perfection and possibilities of the strategic, because the one thing that the Program discovered is that it is the most successful way for a bio-form to survive with the potential of self-reflected consciousness. What a drag to be a bio-form! Think about all those other bio-forms that have to die for other species to live. How much time you spend a day dealing with the dilemmas of what it is to be a bio-form, and how many strategies you have to develop to survive. We humans were the best that any kind has ever seen. So what is the Rave?

If you deal with a bio-form, you can't give up strategy. Because if you are not strategic, you are going to die. The conscious Penta is the great strategic creature. It will look after it parts. The human Penta is not conscious. Therefore, we are not locked into it. We go in and out of Pentas all our lives. We are constantly morphing like lava-lamps. We are all components in a vast life Program, and as components – evolutionary speaking – we are learning how to come together. We are moving towards a commonality, a oneness. Not we humans, of course.

After the Night of Brahma, when the Personality Crystal will come and penetrate the universe – similar to our own Personality Crystal penetrating the physical womb – then, and only then, will everything be seeded with, what in fact is, *one* Personality.

We are the work of a vast consciousness. The neutrino ocean spreads across the entire shore of the known universe. It's everywhere. This whole thing is nothing but a vast consciousness. And it's still a form, working and preparing.

How do you prepare for shared consciousness?

How do you prepare for the release, surrender and acceptance to give up individual consciousness for a larger and greater Personality?

We are about to see the first experiment on that track. An experiment where the individual means nothing. Totally dependent and locked-in, yet, free of any resistance.

While humans have been burdened by homogenisation, the Raves will be the perfection of it. Homogenisation was the beginning of turning us into Raves. Just think of religions, these "homogenising institutions". Just to get us to the Rave.

When over one billion people get down on all fours at the same time? Every day? You are pointing at the Rave. If you look at any day's transit, you can see how the Program alters what the world sees. This is moving us towards the Rave. That's why it is so difficult for people to break away from homogenisation, because it's the future. God and religion are tools to fuse consciousness into a single view, to give everybody the God they can surrender to. But we can't give our self fully to anything, because we are intended only to have our own Authority.

The Rave will not need God. It has its Penta. They are not looking for anything. They are not reasoning anything. They are not in charge. They are helpless, perfect and without choice. I'm not even sure they will be conscious of their own existence. The Penta will. You have this wonderful "god head". This is what this whole God story is. It was always written into our genes.

We've been conned, and all for one goal: is it possible to meld consciousness?

Global Cycles and a Brief History of the Round

Date	Epoch	1	2	7	13	15	10	25	46	Cross								
16513-16102 BC	The Lock	44	24	33	19				46	Cross of the Vessel of Love								
16101-15688 BC	The Key	1							6	Cross of Eden								
15689-15278 BC	The Key	28	27	31	41				36	Cross of the Four Ways								
15277-14866 BC	The Key	50	3		26				22	Cross of the Unexpected								
14865-14454 BC	The Key	32	42	56	60				45	Cross of Rulership								
14453-14042 BC	The Key	57	51	62	61				63	Cross of Consciousness								
14041-13630 BC	The Key	48	21	53	54				37	Cross of Laws								
13629-13218 BC	The Key	18	17	52	58				16	Cross of Planning								
13217-12806 BC	The Lock	46	25	15	10				40	Cross of Maya								
12805-12394 BC	The Key	6	36	12	11				59	Cross of the Sleeping Phoenix								
12393-11982 BC	The Key	47	22	45	26				55	Cross of Penetration								
11981-11570 BC	The Key	64	63	35	5				20	Cross of Tension								
11569-11158 BC	The Key	40	37	16	9				34	Cross of Contagion								
11157-10746 BC	The Key	59	55	20	34				8	Cross of Service								
10745-10334 BC	The Key	29	30	8	14				14	Cross of Explanation								
10333-9922 BC	The Lock	4	49	23	43				49	Cross of Service								
9921-9510 BC	The Lock	13	13	2	1				23	Cross of Explanation								
9509-9098 BC	The Key	33	19	24	44				15	Cross of the Vessel of Love								
9097-8686 BC	The Key	31	41	27	28				12	Cross of Eden								
8685-8274 BC	The Key	56	60	3	50				45	Cross of the Four Ways								
8273-7862 BC	The Key	62	61	42	32				35	Cross of the Unexpected								
7861-7450 BC	The Key	53	54	51	57				16	Cross of Rulership								
7449-7038 BC	The Key	39	38	21	48				20	Cross of Consciousness								
7037-6626 BC	The Key	52	58	17	18				8	Cross of Laws								
6625-6214 BC	The Lock	15	10	25	46				23	Cross of Planning								
6213-5802 BC	The Key	12	11	36	6				2	Cross of Maya								
5801-5390 BC	The Key	45	26	22	47				24	Cross of the Sleeping Phoenix								
5389-4978 BC	The Key	35	5	63	64				27	Cross of Penetration								
4977-4566 BC	The Key	16	9	37	40				3	Cross of Tension								
4565-4154 BC	The Key	20	34	55	59				42	Cross of Contagion								
4153-3741 BC	The Key	8	14	30	29				51	Cross of Service								
3741-3330 BC	The Key	23	43	49	4				21	Cross of Explanation								
3329-2928 BC	The Lock	2	1	13	7				25	Cross of the Vessel of Love								
2927-2506 BC	The Key	24	44	19	33				36	Cross of the Four Ways								
2505-2094 BC	The Key	27	28	41	31				22	Cross of the Unexpected								
2093-1682 BC	The Key	3	50	60	56				47	Cross of Rulership								
1681-1270 BC	The Key	42	32	61	62				63	Cross of Consciousness								
1269-858 BC	The Key	51	57	54	53				37	Cross of Planning								
857-446 BC	The Key	21	48	38	39				57	Cross of the Sleeping Phoenix								
445-34 BC	The Key	17	18	58	52				54	Cross of Penetration								
33 BC-378 AD	The Lock	25	46	15	10				21	Cross of Tension								
379-790 AD	The Key	36	6	11	12				30	Cross of Contagion								
791-1202 AD	The Key	22	47	26	45				49	Cross of Service								
1203-1614 AD	The Key	63	64	5	35				38	Cross of Explanation								
1615-2026 AD	The Key	37	40	9	16				58	Cross of Planning								
2027-2438 AD	The Key	55	59	34	20				10	Cross of the Sphinx								
2439-2850 AD	The Key	30	29	14	8													
2851-3262 AD	The Key	49	4	43	23													
3265-3674 AD	The Lock	13	7	1	2													

Epoch ←→

Round ←→

146

The Mechanics of this knowledge are so special. It allows us to see in so many different ways. It's not about being a fortune-teller in any sense. It's more about the logic of the knowledge that guides you. We are caught in a vast mechanical process in which we are truly helpless. From the last chapter, we came to understand the evolutionary movement towards *oneness*.

There are many things, like the unity of consciousness of a vast totality, that we can never grasp, but we can appreciate the Program moving its way, billions of years by billions of years. We all have to accept the limitation of our time and our place. It is clear that the human race is in the crowning point of its existence, which unfortunately is also the precipice of an abyss. From 2027 onwards, it is simply about "falling" for us. The Program is steam-rolling past us. This is our last opportunity, over the next 1,300 years, for those who incarnate as humans to fulfil the potential of what it is to be us. What we are about to examine is the far reaching and extraordinary power of the Program. It is not some kind of abstract. We are dealing with logic and movement of this force, of the Program.

A lot of beings assume the Program is out there somewhere, but if you look at the Graph, you see that natural ability for receptivity. We have receptors that we need. We are imprinted at birth with some specifics, but we also need receptors otherwise we can't partake in the life process. We have receptors to the Program, to the deepest level of programming. Each of us carries them inside of us.

When we look at our Love Centre, we have to recognise that this is the abode of the Magnetic Monopole, which holds us together in the illusion of our separateness. It is the ultimate instrument of the Program, the great mystery that creates life, and it is yet to be recognised and established scientifically. Within it, lies the answer of how the quantum and relativistic state actually operate together. Not only does it hold us together, but it also moves us in our geometry. It's the coordinator of billions and billions of elements of life on this planet, and the most unbelievable dance one can imagine.

It is the Monopole that guarantees that no two objects occupy the same place at the same time. Its domain is the Love Centre, and this is what's meant by *identity*.

What humans understand as identity is usually the Desire Centre, the *I*, the *I am* speaking.

The identity of the Love Centre is something beyond. It's a higher principle of coordination. It's out of our Love Centre that everything about us is controlled. There is a magic and beauty in the Gates of the Love Centre. It's a theme of holding things together. You look at the spider's web of what's holding the whole thing together. It is what locks *us* to the Program.

The Precession of the Equinox

If you look at the most important aspects in a human chart, they are the Sun and the Earth. They represent 70% of our programming. In the Mandala Wheel, they form a Cross at 88 degrees.

The difference is that Crosses for the larger Program are linked to the precession of the equinox, not the Sun, and are fixed Crosses at 90 degrees. We humans are the mutation and life, and therefore we are 88 degrees. The outer Program is not. The spokes here are fixed at 90 degrees.

The Round of Civilisation – The Lock and the Key

There are 48 Global Cycles in a Round of 19,776 years. Currently, we are living in what's called the *Round of Civilisation*, which began 16,101 BC and will end 3,675 AD. One Round has six Epochs, within which we have different Cycles. At the moment, we live in an Epoch that began 379 AD and will go to the end of life on this planet.

The Global Cycles work by what we call the *lock and key system*. Every eight movements back in the Wheel, the *lock* changes. If you look at the illustration, you have to see that the *lock* and *key* always have a special relationship. The *lock* for the current Epoch are the following Gates:

- 10 *The Nature*
- 1   *The Example*
- 46 *The Temple*
- 7   *The Leader*
- 15 *The Pattern*
- 2   *The Plan*
- 25 *The Way*
- 13 *The Witness*

At the moment of writing, the equinox is in Gate 37 (*key*), which has a special relationship with the Gate 25 (*lock*). So that would mean the *Way* (Gate 25) of our times is characterised by

Gate 37. It would also mean that if you have Gate 25 in your chart, you are going to be connected with someone who has Gate 37.

In 2027, the *Way* will become Gate 55. It's basically about two wheels moving against each other. An inner and an outer Wheel.

Gate 10 stands for *The Nature* or our behaviour. At the moment, Gate 10 has Gate 9, which stands for focus and concentration. It stands for the industrial age, school systems, and organised governments, all because of this.

This Cycle began in 1615 and will end 2027.

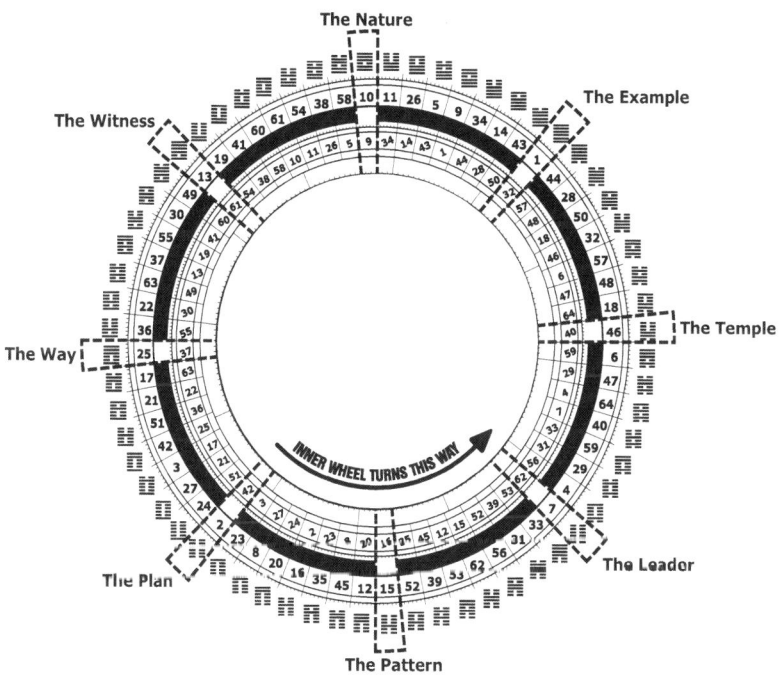

So, when you are looking at the Love Centre, you are looking at the *lock*. This is what locks us to the Program. It's what's holding everything into this evolutionary movie. It's inside of us. There are rotating *keys* that fit into these *locks*. They represent the Cycle of the evolutionary process. If you look at the *lock* that says the *Way*, you are also holding a *key* for any given Cycle that fits.

At the moment, we have the *Cross of Planning*. And there we have the 37th Gate, which will shift to the 55th *key* in 2027. This specific *lock* and *key* has been there for a long time. Hundreds of years. The *Way* has been dominated by the family. You can see there is no *single Way*. There are *many Ways*. They represent an evolutionary pattern because that's what the Wheel is. If you look at the lower couplet of Hexagrams in an Epoch, at the space on the Wheel between the 10th and 19th Gate for example, you notice they are all the same. This is the common theme. They all carry the same chemistry for that Epoch. It's a subtle progression on the theme of *Nature*. You are looking at evolution here, the way it works. It's as extraordinary and beautiful of a perspective that any human being has ever been privileged to have.

Our *Way* for hundreds of years was the *Way* of the family. What did we get from it? All our institutions, our communities, our city-states, our nations, and our concerns for each other. And everything is a bargain, a contract. It's all about what the citizen owes the state, what the state owes the citizen, what the citizen owes the priest, and what the priest owes the citizen. This is the Communal Circuit, after all, that the 37th Gate belongs to. On the other side, you can see the *key* to the *Temple* in Gate 46 is the 40th Gate. What's interesting in the *Temple* is the last 400 years of the spiritual denial; the emergence of scientific thought to challenge spirituality is part of this Cycle.

I am somebody that has the 25th Gate in his Design. I am a *lock* person, but I don't have the 37th. Whenever I meet a 37th, that relationship is a very important one. The *key* goes in the *lock*, and this process that the Program demands at this time in the turning of the Wheel at this place, at this point in evolution, comes out.

The Cycle of the Sleeping Phoenix

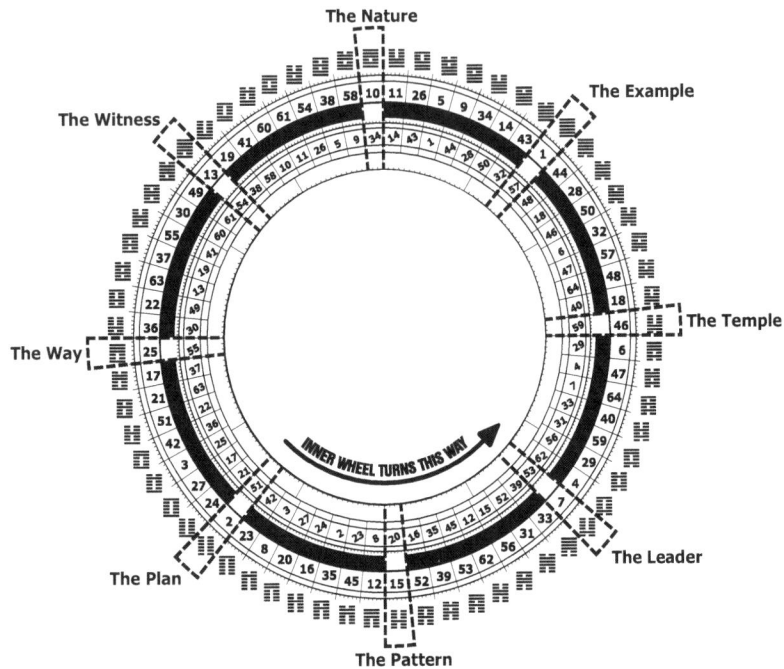

The carpet is slowly but surely being pulled out from under our feet as a human species. It's not like a vast plague is coming. It's kind of a joke, as it isn't coming from the outside. It's built-in on the inside. We sort of become useless, if I can say so with my black sense of humour. We have had this incredible fertility since approximately 1960, but it's just the Program and it will run its full course by 2027. Then the juice will peter out. There will be a lack of fertility in all kinds of ways. We are entering into a deeply dark period.

When you look at the direction of a Cycle, you always start with the trident. To understand the general movement of a Cycle, you start with the 2nd Gate, the *Plan*. This is the place of the Monopole, and it has three variations of how it will play out. The 7th, the 1st, and the 13th Gates. This is the trident, a three-pronged spear. The *Plan* is kind of a nine-dimensional road map. Since the beginning of the 17th century, we had the 42nd Gate as our *Plan*.

When we think about the end of humanity and the coming of the Rave, you can see, we really have the right Gate. It is all about ending things. This is an "end-Gate", not a "beginning-Gate". The *Plan* says that we will reach our maturation, and we will end our Cycle. The 51st Gate that will come is about bringing shock. If you tell humanity in 2027, it is all going to fall apart, they are not going to believe you. But this is what this knowledge is, to prepare a few for what's coming.

There is going to be a shattering of the vanity of humanity that the *Plan* will bring. How nice it is to be in a Cycle to finish things.

In 2027, it all changes. We will not have that *support* anymore. From 2027 on, the Program is not interested in humans. It carries nothing that is specifically for humanity. It is all for what's coming, the Rave. It's an improvement, after all, in the evolutionary sense. We are going to have a shattered world for hundreds of years. Think about the fall of the Roman Empire. Think about the span from 400 AD to 800 AD and how a trans-European, sophisticated society dissolved and broke apart. How things were lost and things were gained. How everything changed. We are going to leave behind the sweet

Communal theme of "I'm going to look after you". This was the *Cross of Planning*, the *Cycle of Planning*. The greatest Cycle that we as a species have ever had. There has never been a greater moment in our history for us humans.

Because this is the end, none of these themes will have any power when we cross the line over 2027. All these institutions we've built, the way in which we have learnt to live with each other in rat mazes, in dense overpopulated environments without butchering each other all the time. Because at least the trucks arrive with food every day. Day in and day out.

Have you ever imagined what it takes for New York City to have breakfast? Do you have any idea what this *Cycle of planning* has done to us? How incompetent human beings are at the most basic level? That their chances of survival, when the electricity goes out, is nil? In an age that is coming, where there is nobody naturally inclined to support you anymore?

Evolution is like carbon-monoxide. A sneaky bastard, and then – boom! Gone! Although it won't disappear overnight. We have all these human beings who have been conditioned by the *Cross of Planning* that will resist the change. They still want to hold on to the United Nations, governments, and labour unions.

Think about when there is no breakfast for Mexico City. What will people do when the support mechanisms break down? When there is no police force, no schools? Do you think this is all going to last because it is here now? This has all been for us. Raves won't need it. They will not need institutions. All this has been built for us in the last 400 years. We will be lucky if the internet survives the next 100 years.

I love the way the Wheel turns. The end of humans and the beginning of Raves. They will lead. It is written in the map. There is a new beginning, and it's different. It's in the coming *Cycle of the Phoenix* that it is going to shake out. You will see the breakdown of the human infrastructure, of fertility, and the Raves will emerge. It is a time of de-stabilisation when there is no more protection for us. Most children today grow up with the illusion of *planning* as their security blanket, that there will be jobs and an organised world in front of them. It's what we have gotten used to. It's like a junkie with its fix. Boy, will we have to go cold-turkey! Not everybody can handle that. It's a vast change. It's not like in 2027 a curtain will be drawn. We are already in it, crawling towards it.

Everything will be for the Raves. It will not bother them that the cities are in ruin. They don't "see". It's not important for them what all that is. They will have their own world, being busy with their own thing: the conscious Penta. But humans will not have such an advantage.

Our world and our movement are driven by detail, driven by facts, and driven by the logic of all of that. It's the way we have been moved, what we follow in that sense, even if some of the facts are lies. The *collective* facts and details have been our leading forces in implementing this plan. You can't imagine something more different from the 62nd Gate than the 53rd that's coming. It has no detail or facts. All it wants to do is start something. There is only a beginning. It doesn't have any facts yet. From one end comes a new beginning.

For us humans, it will mean to be a survivor, to survive the shock. To be a survivor who lives on the spirit of its unique accomplishment. I don't fear for our children. I only fear that there will be so many who will be so disoriented in this great shifting that they will suffer unnecessarily in a life that can still be what any life can be. A life of beauty and grace, a life of unique, differentiated truth.

To be human is no longer a privilege, but an obligation to our own species that it can leave this plane with grace. This is what the knowledge is for, especially in 100 years or 200 years from now, when the depth of this Cycle begins to work its way, when the remnants of *Planning* will be long gone.

The end on this plane isn't going to be a mystery. Humanity will probably know it is coming, long before it comes. And the Raves will know. It has to with the geometry of the great dance in heaven. Things bang into each other. It is the way things go. We are surrounded by objects, hurtling at incredible speeds that bang into each other, and change trajectory. We have vast dedicated intelligence and computers trying to map as many asteroids as possible, because we know that at least one of them is a potential planet killer. It's not going to be God and his hordes riding down from heaven to fight the great battle against the Devil. This time before the end, the *Cross of Explanation* from 2851–3262, is going to be the only period, where the potential of Rave might actually be seen. There will be enough conscious Rave Pentas, so that they can begin to form at least primitive communities that in a sense will control environments, and through that will expand their cognitive power. This will allow them to build a kind of Maya we cannot grasp.

We will be as unimportant to the lives of Pentas as ants are to us. We only pay attention to ants if they go into the kitchen during the wrong time of the year. You don't want to bump as a human into a "Rave kitchen" at the wrong time of the year. This will be *their* time. We will not have the Rave sensory equipment. We don't fit into their world. They might as well be on another planet. We don't get the same advantage by getting together in a group like the Penta. We can't compete with that.

Your children and grandchildren will go with the punches. They will not carry the same vanity and arrogance that we have. We have been the favourites of our time, and they will be put in their place. Think about those dinosaurs when they had been embraced by the Program for 300 million years. They ruled the world, and it wasn't a world we know. It changes all the time. This is going to be the Program for a world we won't live in. We won't live in the Rave's world, but it doesn't mean that our world will disappear. It only means we have no place in the Rave's world. This is the time to be human, and there is only very little time left. Most of your Crystals will not incarnate again. Less and less humans are going to come in to the world. The Wheel is turning and it's turning against us. It has bigger fish to fry. So this is it. What it takes is the grace to bow down to the form, to surrender to its intelligence, to allow it to live its life, and it will not matter in what age you live in.

The Apocalypse

The word *apocalypse* is not well understood. Some people think it's the end of the world, but the ancient Greek word means *to unveil*, which is why you have the *Revelation of Saint John*. In fact, the apocalypse is the discussion of the end of an age by a messenger. What's coming is not an end, but the turning of the Wheel in a much larger process. This is about the Consciousness Crystals and it has always been about them. They have gone through creation and destruction, embodied in various creations of form and all part of the long evolutionary history of the universe itself. We would have to go through the birth and death of generations of stars before there would even be the elements necessary for our self-reflected consciousness in this form to work. Death is inevitable, transcendent, and the turning of the Wheel.

The end is not the punishment of God. It's just a vast natural process. Nothing is eternal. Everything has a beginning and an end. And nothing stops. There is an end that's coming, and we are moving towards it. You must be a fool to see that there is an end to everything, yet believe there isn't one for our world.

The end of this Round brings what mutation brings on a grand level. There is going to be a culling. There have always been cullings. It's along the theme of *the good will be rewarded, and the bad will be punished*, only that it won't be like this. Crystals have a quality. They can be understood through the four basic principles of yin and yang. The future is all about a deep capacity to integrate. Everything serves a purpose in its time. It's not about being evil. All the yang-yang Crystals are no longer needed in the future and will be annihilated after this Round. These Crystals have been around for 14 billion years. One can't even imagine what they have been through over such a vast space and movement.

One of the oddest stories the Voice told Ra was about the arrival of Neptune into our Solar System. We have an anomaly in our Solar System that has never been fully explained by science. It can be seen in the moons of Uranus, as one of them in particular has been fused together from three different pieces of debris in an instant of incredible heat.

Uranus itself was hit so hard by something that its magnetic poles shifted to its equator. It was also knocked into a full retrograde spin, with its magnetic field on its side, which gave Uranus its enormous electromagnetic whip that it is now whipping around our Solar System. About 2.7 billion years ago, something crashed into the Solar System. What entered was Neptune, which came originally from nearby Dubhe, a star that makes up part of the Four Corners and is 123 light years away from us.

When Neptune entered the Solar System, an earlier culling took place because the Consciousness Crystals were on board. This is how they arrived into our Solar System. Those Crystals that were culled were in a gravitational sense dragged into the orbit of our Sun, and pulled into the central furnace of the Sun. At that moment, the Sun was seeded with consciousness. And according to the Voice, this is where all the yang-yang Crystals will go to after this Round. It's not an instant annihilation. The impact of a culling is the slow release of information.

The Camel and the Dog have been the filtering agents of those that have been culled before. Sacrifice is part of growth. Slowly, Round after Round, the Crystals will be broken down in this extraordinary furnace.

The next bundling of the Consciousness Crystals will be without the yang-yang. And everything changes without this deep penetrating force. All these myths about Judgement Day, the damned, the wicked being punished, going to hell and burning in the fire, are like a slightly distorted B-horror movie of what's really going to happen.

The reality of what is going to happen is simply that the Earth will be hit by an object. This is the way space works. The universe is nothing but things banging into each other. It's the way things are created. According to recent calculations, there are between 7,000 and 25,000 objects of planet-killer size that could, depending on their own interactions, hit the Earth. When you think about the asteroid-belt that's between Mars and Jupiter, you have to see that these objects are constantly banging into each other, and by doing so, change their geometry. Thousands of tons of debris hit the Earth every day from the sky. They are just out there, waiting for its moment in the great movement of things. If you look at all those planets that don't have atmospheres or the Moon, you can see all the pockmarks.

Do you remember when Shoemaker-Levy banged into Jupiter? That would have destroyed Earth. If humanity is fortunate, it will only have about 40 to 70 hours warning. It's not like they will be able to predict it. It will just happen, and that will be it. Not necessarily what old prophets wanted to see. The only battle that is there at the end, which the prophets misread, is the 1,000 years that Raves and humans have to deal with each other on the road to the end. It's not the forces of God meeting the forces of Satan on some great battlefield.

All the Consciousness Crystals, no matter if they ever incarnated or not, except the yang-yang, will move on. All those souls will be saved. For another day, for another form, for another journey. There will be no great answer at the end. The world will not go to its end in an act of beauty and glory. There will just be fear for most. Well done, and next. And next it shall be. And the yang-yang will perish. And all life on this planet will die. Whatever is rooted in the genetic code will be destroyed. There will be no escape. None. It will be a clean slate after this.

The Consciousness Crystals will bundle, as they always have. The very shock of the planetary encounter will create the impetus for the bundling. It will take place around the Design Crystal bundle.

When I described the process and moment of biological death in us, we talked about how the Magnetic Monopole and the Design Crystal together leave the body at the moment of physical death. And the death of life on this planet will be when the Design Crystal bundle literally leaves the planet. It will get sort of whacked out by what's hitting the Earth. It carries with it the zillions and zillions of Monopoles. They will "call" all the Crystals and pull them around the bundle. And then the bundle will be in movement again – after being here on Earth for quite a long time. If you can imagine it, you would sort of see it like a sperm. This blob with a tail. And the tail is all the yang-yang Crystals. They are not part of the core and the central configuration. The bundle will move towards the Sun. It will swing around the Sun, leaving behind all the yang-yang, taking them to their place of annihilation. Then, it continues with its journey. That bundle is selective in which Personality Crystals it is carrying, in the way they and their layers are arranged. It all has to do with Fractals. It would be amazing to see the re-arrangement of all the Crystals around the Design Core. They will be arranged according to the Fractals, the way they were connected to each other from the very beginning, less the yang-yang.

Ra always knew who was yang-yang. It was not something he thought about, but something that just happened. He was also told by the Voice how to see the difference, but he never told anyone, as he could not see the value of doing so. The Sun is also yang-yang. It will die, too.

The Night of Brahma

The Night of Brahma is the return to emptiness, to nothingness. In a sense even beyond nothingness. It's nothing we are in any way familiar with. It carries with it a flavour of frightfulness and fear. This emptiness that every child feels when it ponders its own death. Every child will do it at some point, and they end up in this odd space of not being able to grasp nothingness. Some are frightened and others can be exhilarated by it. I don't think it's actually possible for any of us to comprehend what takes place during the Night of Brahma, in this emptiness.

The more we go into the future, the more we reach a certain level of incompetence within us. Certain things have been revealed, leaving us wondering even what the point of such a thing can be. What's coming can only be a story for now. It can't be anything else. Time will tell.

With all likelihood, it will be an asteroid that will end life on Earth at the end of the Round. There is an asteroid belt between Mars and Jupiter, which seems to be debris of a failed protoplanet. The number of objects there are mind-blowing, and some of them are quite large. Certain scientists are trying to track as many as they can, but it's a hopeless task. The problem is that all these asteroids are constantly banging into each other and therefore changing trajectory. You can see how difficult it is to track something that might end up being the planet killer. It's like a huge billiards table with endless balls. You have almost no predictability.

There is a region in the asteroid belt that is relatively close to us. It's called NEAs (near-Earth asteroids) and they have orbits that cross that of the Earth. Because they are relatively close to us in terms of the size of our Solar System, the actual time of warning we could have is fairly small. There are all these people trying to codify and catalogue all objects in space in order to keep track of them. We always knew that this is in the cards for us. Look at the dinosaurs. They ruled the planet, this huge alien world of reptiles. All the other life forms had to scurry around in the dark hiding from them. Then all of a sudden, there comes an absolutely wonderful rock that causes a nuclear winter, with the Sun blocked out for years and these cold-blooded dinosaurs were gone. Just like that. This is the movie, and it is not a new movie. This is just how the plot works, this is how mutation works. Have you ever seen those incredible photographs of galaxies banging into each other? Unbelievable! This is a vast mutative Program. From our perspective, it seems rather coarse, but then just look inside of you at T-cells banging into and invading a microbe, and then chewing it alive. There is a rock with our number out there, just waiting. Sitting out there in one of these zones.

It will never be about *if*. It's just *when*, and according to the Voice, we have a time frame when this will happen. We never have been given a precise date. I guess it could be pretty amazing to see it happen. The heat, the light, and the sound when it approaches the atmosphere. It would be such an interesting thing to see how fragile everything is, how fragile life is. It is a great mutative step.

*

The striking of the planet will dislodge the Design Crystal bundle, literally throwing it out of the Earth and out of the Earth's atmosphere. You are looking at planetary death in the same way as when you look at human death: the Design Crystal leaving the human body with the Monopole embedded.

When the Design Crystal bundle leaves the environment, all support for life is lost. It doesn't just fire out there on its own. It is not comfortable when it is exposed. That's why it spends its existence deep within the mantle of the Earth. So, what happens when it leaves the Earth is: the Monopoles of the Design Crystal bundle attract all the Personality Crystal bundles and it shrouds itself with all these Personality Crystals. The shrouding that takes place is not random. The Monopoles will call certain Crystals and bundles at certain times.

The Crystals that will be closest to the Design Crystal bundle surface will be yin-yin and the last one on the outer shell will be the yang-yang Crystals. There is a kind of choreography going on.

The consciousness field is moving. The core of the potential of universal consciousness is moving. The Crystals that we all carry have already travelled incredible distances over 14 billion years. It's truly phenomenal to think about it. Within each of us is the history of the whole universe. They are witnesses of it all. This beautiful ball called Earth was just a stop along the way, just a beautiful place to rest and get on with self-reflected consciousness. But it is a temporary abode. There is a whole different form that has to come. When we get to the end of the Round, we come to a point where the experiment can't go any further on this plane. By the time we get to the evolution of the conscious Rave-Penta, we reach the obvious limitation of the bio-form. The bio-form is a problem, no matter how sophisticated you become. It's a deep limitation. There is so much that has to work, so many moving parts. It has to be fed, it is fragile, and you need a certain kind of planet with a certain potential for bio-development. But it can get you only so far. Biology has the problem of a limited life span. There are so many things on Earth that only exist for a moment. Biology is nothing but death. Over and over again. Rub your hand, and you kill millions of cells. We have to pay so much attention to the bio-form and it has to be maintained. It's why the Crystal bundle has to move on, because the Earth is not the right medium for what's coming.

What's coming is not a bio-form at all, at least not in any conceivable way that we can understand it. This is the end of life as we know it. The bio-form has been interesting because of its mutative potential. When you escape the bio-form, you actually leave mutation behind. That's really something to think about. This is what's so incredible about the bio-form. There is this constant reproductive mutation that takes place with every generation. If you go back 2.5 billion years to the beginning of life on this planet, you can see how long it took. Four million years ago, we were not sophisticated and had just figured out how to walk erect. About 200,000 years ago, we were savages. Then 10,000 years ago, we figured out how things grow. Go back 7,000 years ago, we started to write. Think about how long it has taken to develop the infrastructure for self-reflected consciousness. The Program says: "Okay, we've invested 2.5 billion years into this. It was very interesting. Yes, we do get self-reflected consciousness. Very good, but we need to do much better than this. Much more sophisticated, much more efficient." So, it replaces mutation with something quite remarkable, that is a kind of immortality. Relative immortality. No bio-form, no death. No bio-form, no reproduction. It's very different, what's beyond the end on Earth, beyond the closing of the Round. The planet where we are coming from is rare. It has a special environment that was needed for the bio-form, and where we are going is as common as it can be. We leave behind the bio-form and we will become aliens, so to speak. By the time we get to the point of describing where we are going in this book, it is as good as any science-fiction story you could ever imagine.

When the Design Crystal bundle is moving out of the Earth, it is pulling with it all Design Crystals of life on the planet. Things are just going to die in an instant. When this happens? Wow! Talk about a wave! Unbelievable. Death will be everywhere. Zillions of fish dying within moments. It's the life-force perishing. It's the form principle dying. The bundle, as it moves, is tearing all life out of the planet, and as it does that, it layers in the Personality Crystals to create a sheath, to protect itself as it moves through space.

You have to understand: once the Crystals leave the planet, the lights have been turned out. There is no "thinking" and no "seeing". There is no hardware, there is no existence, there is no universe, no unique lives, and there is no unique intelligence. There is nothing. This is the emptiness. But it is not really nothing. Because the Design Crystal bundle and its sheath of Personality Crystals are actually in movement. And everything is about movement. In the magic of the Design Crystal bundle and its Personality sheath leaving the planet, they go on a journey which is a slingshot journey.

The Crystals will go around the Sun, but they will not go back to where they started. You have yin-yin, then yin-yang, then the yang-yin, and then on the outside of the bundle, the yang-yang Personality Crystals. When they will go around the Sun and come within its reach, the outer sheath of the yang-yang will get pulled into the core of the Sun where they will remain until they are annihilated, which ultimately will be until the Sun itself dies.

After going around the Sun, the Crystals will continue their journey towards Jupiter. It will not be their final destination, but it is an important place to go. We already talked about the importance of Jupiter and its four Galilean moons, which in their electromagnetic interaction with Jupiter carry all the information that runs the programming on Earth.

The Galilean Moon Europa

Europa is an extraordinary, absolutely beautiful moon of Jupiter. It has frozen water underneath the surface. Europa is tiny compared to Jupiter. The Crystal bundle and its sheath, after arriving, will run parallel to Europa, caught in the electromagnetic connection and gravitation of Jupiter. It will be caught in there for an incredibly long time. It will move with Europa in its movement, in a sense staying in its shadow as it moves around Jupiter in many cycles. The Voice said it will take 200 million years from the end of this Round to reconstitute life, to reconstitute the consciousness-field. In other words, to put the Consciousness Crystals back into self-reflected forms.

About 200 million years of emptiness. Not that it matters, which is the joke. It's not like anybody is concerned about it or has to wait. And at some moment, when the process is at the right place, at the right time, suddenly it will be there. And suddenly, those Consciousness Crystals with all of their potential, the software that they are, will finally get a new hardware and will begin the end-game process, which will take another two billion years. The universe, the Child, is an enormous entity.

The Crystal bundle will go through an endless dance around Jupiter, taking in the remains of the electromagnetic field. Everything that has transpired in the incarnative Program of humanity can be found in the environment of Jupiter. It's a special future that will be shaped through that dance. In that very emptiness of the Night of Brahma is also the promise. *It* will never know the emptiness when it emerges. It is the outer Solar System that is being prepared for the future. We currently live in a "pat on the back and golden watch time".

"Thank you very much, but we have a new model. It will be ready in a couple of hundred million years, and, oh boy, is that ever going to be cool."

We are building the consciousness of an incredible thing, which is an enormous process. Remember, if the future is not going to be a bio-form, then they cannot count on mutation to make up for bad engineering. It has to be designed properly. The form principle has to emerge correct and for that it will take hundreds of millions of years of preparation.

We are moving towards a trinary Crystal format, a vehicle with three Crystals with one of those coming from the mammalian plane. There is that extraordinary relationship already growing between humanity and mammals. Although they seem inferior in many ways to us, especially in terms of self-reflective consciousness, what they have learnt in relationship to the way in which they deal with environment is something extremely important for the future. We don't understand the deeper purpose of what mammalian evolution has been about, and the Voice never told us, but it's clear that it's special.

The Voice said that the Personality Crystals of mammals are exactly the same as the Personality Crystals of humans. One of the signs indicating this change of a relationship with mammals after 2027 is the breaking of the 19–49 Channel. I think that there is going to be great karmic punishment for the taking of mammalian life after that point. There might be a price to be paid.

What we are really experiencing is the building of the brain of the totality. It's something spectacular to recognise. We are the body-consciousness, the body-intelligence of the whole. This, the universe, is a maturing vehicle that has not yet emerged into the world it belongs. It's all part of creating a single, vast, self-reflected consciousness.

The majority of Personality Consciousness Crystals, when the end of the Round comes, will never leave the Night of Brahma. They will never incarnate because there will be limited seats. There will be certain Personality Crystals that will have a ticket, not all of them human Crystals. And those that don't have a ticket? It will not make any difference to them. There is a grace to understand your place in the movement of things, and it is beautiful just to see these things. We are mental beings, and it is a great struggle after all to deal with the mind, but I think when you engage mind in such beauty, it's hard for it to stumble back into the folly of being stupid.

Oberon and the Reconstitution

Oberon is so different to anything else in the Solar System. All of the moons of Uranus are named after characters created by William Shakespeare or Alexander Pope. Oberon is the king of the fairies in *A Midsummer Night's Dream*. Even all the names of places on Oberon are named after characters from Shakespeare. It's an extraordinary anomaly in the naming of things in our Solar System. As we already heard, the Crystal bundle is in a totally different configuration for the first time in a long time. As a matter of fact, certain Fractals no longer exist with the stripping of the yang-yang Crystals.

The Crystals are going around Jupiter in a parallel orbit to Europa for millions of years. It is the Night of Brahma, the time of preparation for the reconstitution. What is taking place in that process is not something that any of us could possibly grasp. Yet, a 200-million-year Night of Brahma in a 15-billion-year process is kind of a little nap. After all, an important transformation is taking place. It's the information of the Galilean moons that is carried forward by all of this. The moons themselves will not survive the entire process, which will take two billion years. By then, we will also begin to see the death of the Sun. It will gobble up the inner planets and the moons of Jupiter when it dies. That's why the information must be passed on in the 200-million-year orbit around Jupiter.

Fractal lines are nothing but hierarchical structures. Every time that there is a culling and shifting of the fundamental components, there has to be a realignment of the Fractal. There is something bizarre in this, as this is a unique stage in the history of the movement. For 14 billion years, the Centre Crystals have always been part of the migration of the Crystal bundles. But they will not be going forward. They are going to be left off and annihilated, too. There will be no Centre anymore. A new hierarchy is being established. For 14 billion years, there has always been a central Fractal line, a Centre that was never in the middle, Fractals that were long and short. The Crystal bundle is realigning itself, and we don't know how. When you wake up from Brahma's Night, there will be a completely new movie, but the Consciousness Crystals can't stay there. It's time to move on. Any event like that can only be initiated by a violent act. Something will bang into something, and this will send the Crystal bundle to what is going to be its final journey. It is going to the moon Oberon, one of the major moons of Uranus.

We already heard about the moons of Uranus, when Neptune banged into Uranus as it arrived into our Solar System. One of these moons is called Miranda, and it looks kind of pasted together. As a matter of fact, it's one the most extraordinary objects we have in our Solar System, because it is a moon made up of three different parts. One part looks like a normal cratered moon, the other part looks kind of spongy, and the third part is kind of gouged and full of runny stuff. The three parts are fused together. In order to fuse chunks of rock you have to have absolutely incredible heat, in an event that took place two billion years ago. Ra was told that Oberon and the main moons of Uranus came along with Neptune. They are, in fact, components of what was once a larger Neptune.

Oberon is an incredibly cold place. We would never endure

such a place. It is Moon-like in its nature. It actually looks so much like our Moon that it has the nickname of being its twin. They have approximately the same mass, they look very similar, and have the same kind of surface features. This will be the home for the Consciousness Crystals for two billion years. It's a shorter period than the one we had on Earth. The environment isn't going to be necessarily important, other than the fact that it is incredibly cold. It's necessary for the form principle that will emerge on Oberon, but it is going to be different. Every idea that we ever had about what life is will be over now. To be honest, we would not recognise the new form, the Eron, as a "life". You wouldn't know how to. You can recognise it as a "science-fiction concept" of consciousness, but not as a life. It will bear no association to life as we understand it. The Eron is not a bio-form. You might say, the Eron is wired, rather than genetic. The whole principle of life is different. Anything on Oberon that could be of value to a human is meaningless. It doesn't look like a friendly neighbourhood, but this isn't going to be a world where anything will ever be built. This is a world in which the surface will never be touched.

When the Crystal bundle moves around Oberon, the Personality Crystal sheath will break off, and only when it is completely unfolded will the Design bundle go into the core of it. This will be the same construct as we understand that the Consciousness Crystals operated on Earth. The only difference is what will be constructed, and because it is not a bio-form, it will have extreme longevity. It will not only survive in form for the next two billion years, but perhaps for hundreds of billion years and beyond. We are talking about something that is non-reproductive. Something that we understand as reincarnation will no longer exist.

There is no way to call this "life". Life and death are the same thing. They are one. We are talking about a form principle that is inanimate. It is not alive. There will only be a certain percentage of the Personality Crystals that have made the journey and will be able to enter into form – only a small number. The others will never again enter into form. They will be in a permanent state of nonexistence filtering, similar to the Crystal bundles that exist around Earth now.

It's a long-term program to get to a place of specialisation. Those incarnating into Eron, they are highly specialised. They are on the Fractal for the "big ride". All the way. They are, in essence, the essential components of the Design Crystal of the totality. That's, in fact, what all those Crystals are anyway. They are all aspects of the Design Crystal of the totality. And it is here that the Design Crystal is going to lock its Program in, lock its vehicle program in.

There are trillions of billions of trillions of Crystals, but there will only be millions that will incarnate. The vast majority never will. It is not that they will be without value. They carry the consciousness field as a specific filtering agent, and they always will be part of what is the on-going process, but never truly be a component of it. They are not destined to be part of the Eron.

It's an interesting transition, that movement. First, the bundle leaving Earth, then leaving the yang-yang behind, this long reshuffling process without a Centre, and finally this movement to Oberon. This slow spreading out of the Personality sheath, then the Design going in, and eventually, the beginning of the orchestration of the event. Some kind of vast seeding.

Our uniqueness as humans is determined by time. For example, our birth time. We have a different alignment to different forces, because we arrive at different times in different places. The thing that is so incredible about the reconstitution of Oberon is that it will take place in a moment. All at once. One birthday. This is what we talk about when we talk about homogenisation. It is the future in a way that is hard to imagine. These are components in a greater component. The whole is always going to be greater than the sum of the parts. The Crystals that we carry are, in fact, the body-intelligence of the totality. They transmit into the neutrino ocean into space at the speed of light, and it never stops. The totality is filled with their process, and by the time they are reconstituted on Oberon that is something that can become ultimately a two-way street. This totality, this is our body. If it is our body, it is not simply here to move *us*. We are here to move *it*. We are here to maintain *it*.

It is going to be a selected crew, organised at Jupiter, riding along with Europa. This is where the actual selection process is all arranged. And then a couple of million years to get to the point where it is established. It's metaphysics. How it takes place is hard to imagine, but it certainly takes place in the physical world. It's a real process. It's just slow, like a glacier. Little bit by little bit, things fall into place. By the time they get to Oberon, it's already all laid out in the dance, in the movement. The Monopoles will release the Personality Crystals into the gravitational field of Oberon. Similar to when they let go of the yang-yang for the dive into the Sun. And it is the Monopole that drives its way to the core with the bundle itself.

If you look at all the science-fiction stories and movies of humans, they are all distortions of the human spirit. They are never really alien. What they imagined wasn't really rooted in the alien at all. When I think about the Eron, I really recognise an alien. It's as alien as alien can be. Ra said he reached his level of incompetence as far as this goes, although he has been given the Design of the Eron, which we will look at briefly in the final chapter. He said the encounter was a long story that went on and on. It was the story of the Consciousness Crystals that he was given during the first day. It started off with the Big Bang and he was already enormously drained when it eventually got to this part of the story. And it just kept going and going.

He was given ways to translate the mechanism of the Eron, but that doesn't mean he knows what it possibly can be like. He has actually seen them, as the encounter itself was also extremely visual. Eron are not robots. They have consciousness at a deep level, but they will not in a sense understand where they came from. They are born all at the same time and have a fresh start. Ra said he always loved a good story, and the Voice was the best storyteller he ever met, and that's what he enjoyed so much. He was just taken away by the beauty of the story.

It's a dance and a magical thing. Whatever contribution any one of us ever made, will never disappear. Streaming out of us all the time, in every direction. Nothing is ever lost.

The Eron

No feelings, crisis or change. No hunger.
No judgement, correction or talent. No taste.
No openness. No outside that is inside.
No throat, no voice or mind.
No death.

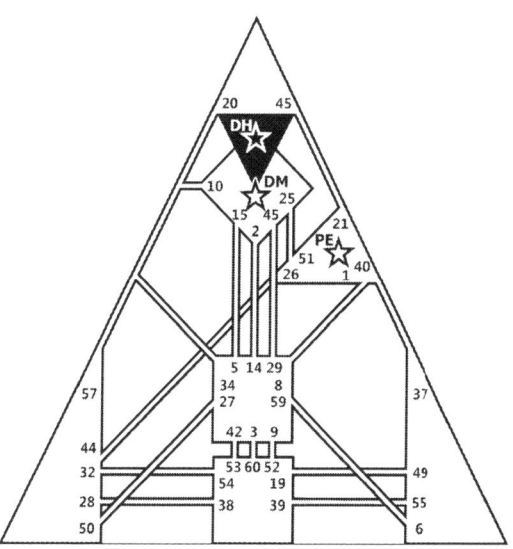

One of the things that struck Ra deeply at the time when he was given the knowledge was the Design of forms. Not just the focus on humans, but all these other forms. It would become a kind of pattern in the revelation. Day after day, there was some kind of form that was being presented. To be in a mad situation, and then on top of that have mad subjects, is bizarre. Ra said that it's very difficult to explain how this is and to be in such a thrall to that kind of an experience, with this otherworldly intelligence going on and on about something that will be hundreds of millions year away in the future. There was a part of Ra asking : "What for?"

He never knew what it is for. He guessed that there are certain Crystals that will ride in these vehicles, and any information that touches them will leave some kind of effect that is in essence information, in whatever way this can possibly work. The beginning stuff was a necessary ingredient to understand the construct of how things are now. But the future? The Eron? Oberon? Orbiting 200 million years around Europa? You can only look at it as a story.

According to the Voice, the Eron is the foundation of the expression of the totality. We are components of that foundation. That foundation is a single life. By saying such a thing, it is impossible to understand what has been just said. We don't know what context to place that in. We understand "life" in a limited way. It's difficult to understand the universe as "one life", as an *it* and not as a collection of things. It's not *within* the illusion that defines it, but what is *beyond* it that defines it. What will define the illusion for this entity is impossible to say or imagine. You can call it the ring-pass-not, an expression from the 19th Century.

When we begin to get to the Eron, we begin to get to a truth. In order for the bundle to leave Europa, an event has to take place. It is a spectacular event. We celebrate it, in fact. In the microcosm, in our little lives.

The Arrival of the Single Personality into the Totality

First, you have to understand that Ra tricked us when he first said we carry a Personality and Design Crystal. He did this on purpose, and we already talked about this in the chapter about the story of the Consciousness Crystals. Both Consciousness Crystals are in essence a Design Crystal. What we refer to as Personality is just another kind of Design Crystal. There are no real Personality Crystals (yet). They are, in fact, a kind of "training vehicle" to get the programming right. All in preparation for the single Personality of the totality when it will arrive. What we call Personality Crystal in the human form is a Design Crystal that has the task of testing if self-reflected consciousness in form is possible. We are testing the infrastructure, so one day when the real Personality arrives in the Eron it will have a working vehicle. We are a Design Crystal taking the seat for the Personality, which isn't here yet and when we die all of us go back to being a Design Crystal.

What does the Design Crystal do in the microcosm of the foetus? It does the work, together with the Monopole, of building the vehicle, building something specific. Everything about that vehicle, our body, is that it is being built to house the potential of self-reflected consciousness, which is going to emerge through being able to receive the Personality Crystal. Not only to receive it, but actually call it. It's the Magnetic Monopole of the foetus that calls in the Personality Crystal.

That Crystal bundle that's there at Oberon is at some point ready. And its readiness is the readiness of the totality to receive its single Personality. The universe is an "it". We don't know what this "receiving" is going to be like on a cosmic scale. We have no idea. A kind of mini Big-Bang in a way. We don't know where it's going to happen, where the totality is going to be penetrated. It will be penetrated from the outside, and at a cosmic scale that we can't know. What we do know is that the ripple effect from that will disengage the Crystal bundle from Europa, and will ultimately bring about the destruction of the Galilean moons. This will be quite a thing. When the Personality on a cosmic level penetrates the totality, the universe, it is going to shatter. But this time it is going to shatter in a way that's hard to understand.

When the Design Crystal shattered, every single aspect was *unique* and only one aspect, the centre aspect, was a microcosm of the totality. But the real Personality Crystal will shatter *perfectly*. Every Crystal-facet will be the microcosm of the whole. Every one of those will be an exact mirror. They will be in essence *all* Centres, and will be called into the Eron vehicle. They are not simply going to be called into the Eron by a Design Crystal and a Monopole. There will be *two* Crystals there calling them in. One of them is what we used to think of Personality. These Personality Crystals as we understand them in humans, which are in fact Design Crystals, will then become the infrastructure, the "brain program" for the *real* Personality.

Every Eron will have the *same* Personality. This is the mechanism for establishing the unique universal Personality of the totality, which is going to take another two billion years. Two billion years until the totality is ready to be born. Born into something we don't know. These two billion years are the equivalent to the three months before the actual birth of a human foetus.

The Eron is an (almost) eternal form. It is unlike anything we can grasp as "life". Oberon is going to be the core of the brain of the totality. The brain of the totality is vast in terms of the star field, and full of its own filtering and initiating of the neutrino ocean. The very core of this cosmic brain will be on the surface of Oberon, its central control mechanism.

The Design Crystal is not only responsible for maintaining the life of its own form, but also for the development of the life of the totality. Providing it with the infrastructure, it will need to demonstrate its relative cognition on whatever plane this is going to be.

We are talking about the potential of the Personality to be plugged in to the collective consciousness that has been our development. The Crystals, as they have lived through humanity, are those that will live through Eron and they will in their process be very much part of the physical life of the totality. We cannot know or understand what life it will be on the outside, just as we cannot imagine such a thing from the inside where we are. It isn't possible. And whatever it will be, what will be its life span? Say, 100 billion years? Or 200 billion years? Does any of that matter?

However long it will be, it will only be possible if the vehicle can be maintained. It will be *our* Design Crystals that filter the possibility of what the totality can be (Oberon is going to be the core of the cosmic Design). It will not only filter it, but it will not filter without influence. This is when the Crystals begin to take intelligent control of the vehicle. Not just simply going through patterns, controlled through an outer Program as we go through and struggle with. The Crystals will *become* the Program, as well as *being* programmed.

"Cold" doesn't describe how cold it is on Oberon. It's hard to duplicate such a thing in laboratories. It is far away from the Sun. And even as the Sun goes through its final billion years of its life, it will never get to a point where that coldness will ever disappear. It is absolutely essential. No living thing that we understand could live on Oberon. We are dealing with an object that is very close to a huge planet, Uranus, and its whipping electromagnetic field. So, Oberon is this deeply frozen place trapped in an electromagnetic sea.

Eron is a four-sided object, not five-sided like a pyramid. To be accurate, it has three sides and one face, in the same way as you can think of humans having two sides and one face. But in a sense it will be different. The Circuits operate according to a side and are only homogenised through the face. The illustration you see at the beginning of this chapter is the illustration of the dynamic of the face. That "face" of an Eron is quite something. This object, the Eron, is a small object. It's sort of made of silica. Pure silica, which is the most abundant thing on this planet and it has incredible properties. It's a cold silica object and it's no more than a meter high, with three sides and a face. It never touches the surface of the moon. It hovers on the electromagnetic field. If you could see it, you would see all these triangular shapes, always in movement. Movement that can be controlled. You have an inanimate object, at least as we understand it, endowed with three Consciousness Crystals, on a frozen moon, in an electromagnetic ocean, floating. And their floating has a purpose. Their purpose is a face.

The number of Crystals that have been annihilated, and the real Personality Crystals that arrive later cancel each other out. All of these levitating Erons have a Program that will take about a billion years out of the two billion-year process. It is literally to lock into a sphere that surrounds the moon, a huge Crystal ball. All of those Erons are going to work out a mathematical Program for linking up and forming this perfect surface, *the* Design Crystal of the totality. But boy, is there a catch!

We humans like "face-to-face". The embrace of lovers, for example. Face-to-face means a lot to us humans. And no matter how sweet the lover, and no matter how important the face-to-face interaction, eventually there is always a relief when it's over and one can turn away. And then you get Erons where face-to-face is more than just a little encounter – it becomes everything. This Program to create the Design Crystal of the totality demands something. It demands a form of bonding that is far beyond anything any human being could imagine. Erons are designed to lock face-to-face. Once they lock, they will never unlock.

You see the grandest of mechanics playing out in the

organisation of this vast consciousness system, and they are components of it. They are finally unified in a oneness through the unique oneness of the Personality Crystals, and the task of creating the sheath, which is not an easy thing. We are not talking about something that is truly inanimate anymore than we are talking about something that is actually life.

The perfection of the consciousness Program is that it doesn't require biology. That's its great triumph. That's what this really is. No feelings, no crisis, no change. No experiential way, no hunger, no judgement, no correction, no talent, no taste, no openness, and no outside that is inside, like noses, mouth and ears. Solid. No throat, no voice and no mind. No mind. This is the ultimate "brain builder". This is no mind. It is building the cosmic brain, organising it. No death.

In the human Graph, the Desire and Service Centres never connect directly. When we look at the Eron, we see something that isn't in a Wheel anymore. It is a whole new construct at work. If you look at the Channel between Desire and Service that provides the immortality of the Eron, you see it is the 8–1. A funny place to find the 8–1. There is no Sharing.

This black Knowing Centre you can see is thrust into the Love Centre. This is symbolic. We know, for example, that at death and conception we have either the separation or coming together of the Monopole and Design Crystal. This is significant in the Eron. Remember, there are three Crystals. The Design Crystal of the Eron (from the mammalian world on our planet) will be locked into the Monopole. They will be embedded together. Our so-called Personality Crystal, which is just another Design Crystal, is going to be pulled into the Love Centre. It's not going to be embedded, but sort of pulled into the orbit of the Monopole and the mammalian Design Crystal. In that space that you see above the black Knowing, will sit the Personality Crystal. But what you can see is that there is no true Solving or Knowing in terms of function. The Gates that are there, that separate the Knowing from the Solving, are the 20 and 45, which is what we would call *Sharing Gates*. But rec-

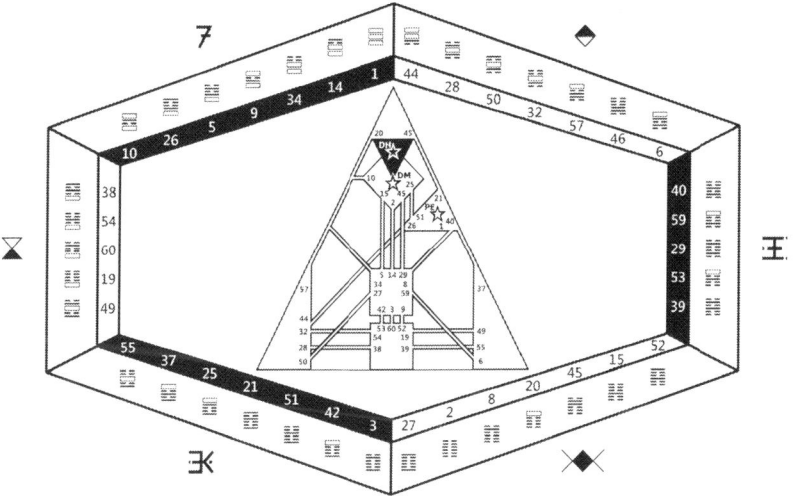

ognise that these are bottom Sharing Gates. They are feeding this mammalian Design Crystal.

There are many things that have to be coordinated in the existence of the Eron. Think about the most common science fiction theme since the advent of the computer. It's A.I., so called artificial intelligence. In other words, to give independent consciousness to an inanimate vehicle. There has been an enormous effort that has taken place, to write the "God code", the "consciousness code" from humans for computers. It is there in *us*, because it is there in our future. But Erons will not be robots. These are not computers. They are conscious forms, and they have a specific Design.

Their primary concern is *movement*, which is navigation. This is why we have a Crystal directly imbedded with the Monopole. The driver and vehicle are aligned as tightly as possible. Everything about the perfection of their process is going to be about their ability to be able to discern with the one element that is really unique and free in a sense. That's what they've inherited from humans. The so-called human Personality Crystal, which now is another Design Crystal. It is going to be up to this Crystal to figure out how or which or where to make that move, to fit in with that other. It is going to be the *discernment consciousness*. And what a job that is! It does it by being able to discern the value and correctness of the other. You can see the benefit derived from the evolutionary process of the human Personality Crystals, learning all of that by playing the part of Personality in order to be prepared in establishing the framework for that in the Eron. It won't be quick. But then, you don't deal with something that does have a mind. And *that's* its perfection. It does not mean it does not have choices or decision making processes. There also will be conditioning elements. But it is not human.

There is something interesting about them though. They

will have a deeply powerful identity. Each one. And the expression of that will be all in their movement. Imagine this cold, crisp, and dark world in that electromagnetic environment. These small objects floating about, on the hunt, waiting and filtering. All of this in that extraordinary dance to get to this place of coupling. There is the magic progression of faces that will couple, that will lead to sides that will bond, that will lead to the construction of this extraordinary thing: the management hub for the existence of the totality. We have a minimal capacity here to grasp what this is. It goes back to Monopoles, which are so incredible.

Wherever we go in the magic of existence, we are always left with this incredible component. The Monopole. It makes everything happen. It is an extraordinary construct, and here it's at its best, pulling everything together and holding it together. This incredible capacity to align us to our direction, to our movement in space, which we call Love. The Monopoles of Oberon will direct the direction of the totality forever. Its "life" managed from here. And, of course, it's the Monopole that holds us together in the illusion of *our* separateness, and here the Monopole is going to express something fascinating. The one thing that makes it stand out from the other. The Personality Crystal it takes in from human. Here, it will be the illusion of uniqueness. The components have to be able to recognise through difference how they lock together, whether they have found the right face to lock into. When there is one, there will begin to be many, until they are all locked in.

*

The values of the Centres in the Eron, as we know them from humans, will not apply. Everything will carry a different meaning. Just carry with you this image of that truly cold, perfect form for consciousness. It will not eat, does not sleep, has no sex, and does not need to hunt. So much of our time is wasted to keep us alive. The Eron will be a perfect box for consciousness. This is our future, according to the Voice.

We humans are an "inside-story". We are not an "outside-story". The only outside-stories are the illusions we are given in this life, and they are entertaining. But we are an inside-story. We are the machinery. We are the mechanics. We are it now, and we don't know it. It's controlled by the Program. What do you think is going on when trillions of neutrinos are penetrating the entire planet every second? Carrying the information of every single consciousness on this planet, all out into space at every single direction at the speed of light? It's not news out there that something changed at 1781. You travel several hundred light years, and you cover a lot of territory in every direction. We have always programmed the whole, as it programs us. It is a biofeedback, but we are at a stage now, where we have no conscious control over that. The Eron will. It can make things happen in the body, and it has to. It is *our* body. Eron fulfils this understanding.

There will be somewhere around 100 million Erons. Ra said he had an exact number, but he always felt silly with exact numbers. The vast majority of the Crystals that will be in the Eron will be in incarnation when the end comes on Earth, and there will be certain Crystals in bundles that will also be part of the Eron process. The same goes for the mammalian Crystals. The Eron, when it eventually will take control of the body, will change the shape of the universe. The only unique aspect that you will have in the Eron is derived from the human Personality Crystal. Nobody should make the mistake of thinking of the unborn universe, "the Child", in terms of human, even if we make some comparisons sometimes. I don't think anyone could grasp what kind of life the universe could possibly be, once it is born. Grasp what kind of world it would be born into. The Voice told Ra that "the universe represents a life, which is not yet born". This was the exact expression he was given. It is the Eron that brings the universe, that unborn entity, to its preparation to be born into its outside world. This entity has a Personality and it is the Eron that provides the neocortex like we have it in humans, on a cosmic scale.

With the Eron, you have to be extremely careful with any Gate interpretation as we know it. Even when humans make movies about aliens, they come up with some sort of bio-form, because this is the only way of life we understand. It's difficult to call the Eron a creature, so it's best to just call it an Eron. We are not dealing with something that incarnated to decarnate, or evolve. Here, we already have the finished solution. Here is the perfection of the form principle. There's no need to go through the mutative experiment. It has properties that are extraordinary and virtually indestructible. It is self-conscious and aware. It is essentially social, and in its own sense, different from every other Eron, but they are orchestrated to operate in

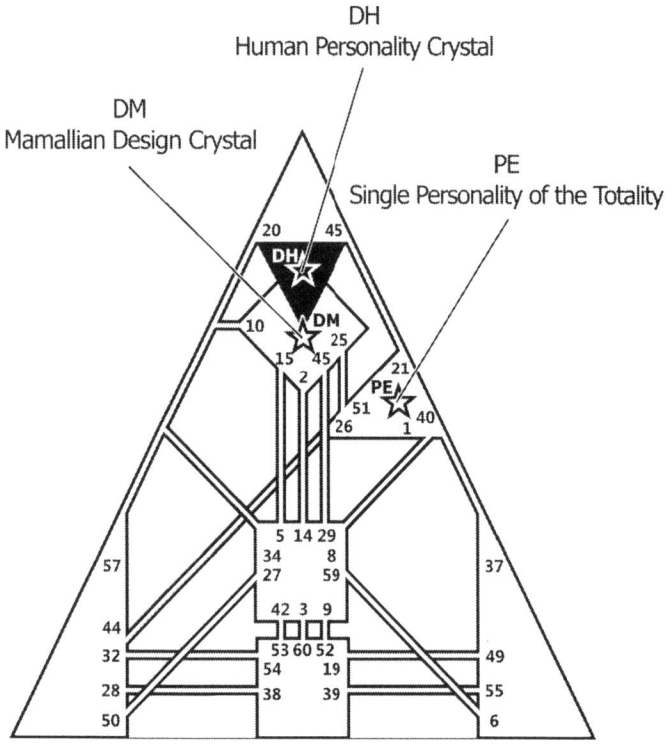

a great harmony. If we are not dealing with the Gates as genetic constructs, then we have to see that their values are different. This is no longer a genetic code. It's a hard-wired code, a permanent way in which this functional construct works. We are struggling to express it within our language. What you see in the Design of the Eron is the schematic of how the neutrino ocean impacts this particular object.

The only Centre that remains, relatively speaking, the same is the Love Centre. There is no Solving Centre as we know it, and there is an odd shaped Desire Centre with an additional Gate.

The Eron is a huge response mechanism. The Service Centre is the core of everything, and it replaces the Sharing Centre where all roads used to meet. What is being generated has more to do with the way in which consciousness is driven. The very value of the Centres themselves is going to be completely different. Any attempt to associate value as we know them is not going to work, and while Ra was told some things in great detail, others were not explained at all.

There is no mind in this creature, as it is not the point. They will be very much influenced by their two variations of awareness. Mind is not their thing. The Eron is not the Personality, but it is going to provide the infrastructure for it. It is not here to be mentally interested in anything. It has other priorities, and of course, it has its identity. It's more connected to geometry and investigation than anything else. You can look at it as a multi-Channel system, linked through a commonality, which is the mechanism that imbues this frozen silica with a consciousness that it works with. The consciousness is alive, and I guess that's the only way it can be expressed. The vehicle is neither alive or dead, it is simply inanimate, but the consciousness is alive within it. It is this grey zone that infuses the consciousness with its vitality. This is the Program being so clever with the form, so precise, that the form just simply houses consciousness. The form itself doesn't require, as we understand it, a consciousness. Everything about this thing is the frequencies that are the result of its Crystal infrastructure.

You can see that we have three Consciousness Crystals. The

Crystal saying DH is the Design Crystal that derives from humans. The DM is the Design Crystals that derived from mammals. PE is the Personality Crystal from the central Crystal system. The PE sits in what we would call the Desire Centre, but we cannot call it this anymore in the Eron, and we don't have a name for it.

All Erons were created at the same time, so it no longer is a matter where Jupiter or Saturn was at the birth. They are programmed and imprinted in a total different way. The knowledge we have about the Eron is obscure, and it's not exactly like our lives depend on it.

There is a great wonder about the "Child", the organising and growth of this cosmic entity. It's going to have a life in the sense that ultimately, whatever that means, it will emerge into whatever dimension it belongs to. When you look at the grey areas of the Eron Design you get a taste of what's beyond. After all, these are components of the great totality that we can see as a singularity.

Every Personality Crystal of the Eron is exactly the same, so in that there is a universal expression of the potential of the cosmic mind that the Eron is designed to support. What you see in the three corners and the Centre with the PE are the parameters that the Eron has to establish in order to be able to offer the Personality the best possible cognitive advantage. It's the blueprint for the coordination for the totality's mind. And don't forget, the Eron is inanimate. It's the *consciousness* that's alive in the Eron, not its body, and it's a *unique* consciousness. That's the miracle.

Understand that there is a destiny for so many beings; that their Consciousness Crystals will take this extraordinary ride in the Eron, beyond the "ring-pass-not", into a dimension that can only be expressed as unimaginable. And to really understand us and our struggle as humans, to finally be able to come to grips through revelation that we are the embodiment of the form principle and its consciousness. If we don't honour these forms – our human forms – we are not going to get the rewards that are here for us. But ultimately, the form principle is not going to mess around anymore. It will get to this point of magical rigidity. This strange thing that we call Eron.

Epilogue

One day, everything that I carried with me in my process, from the time I came into the world, shattered. There was no other way to survive it but to shatter. When that happened I was running an experimental school, and it was years before I would have my "encounter". I had these wonderful kids, about 13 or 14 years old, and was experimenting with their consciousness, I guess. It always struck me that public institutions for education, what they teach in 10 months, you can teach in a month. I was convinced that I could take children of that age, not really children anymore, but teenagers, and open up a different kind of mental and intellectual horizon. There was an open space at the back of my house, it was actually a very small house. But it was a big enough open space that I was able to convert it into a classroom. I only had four kids.

Around that time, I began to go through something that was really very odd. I remember vividly how it started. It was a Sunday and my friend, Frank, who called himself God, was having a luncheon at the house where he stayed. It was late October, and I can remember going out there and there were all these people. About 25 to 30 people, and there were all these tables with food. I kept looking at the food and I kept realising that there was nothing inside of me that wanted any, and there was something wrong with that. There was something wrong with that because I had not had breakfast. There was no reason in the world why I wouldn't be hungry. It was a wonderful display of food. It was a delight. On several occasions plates were put in front of me and nothing happened. So I stopped eating. I didn't go on a fast, because that's what it looked like in a way as I went through the process. But I didn't. I wasn't hungry. That's a very odd thing. I just wasn't hungry. So, I started to go through this process where there was something funny happening to me, and at that point I couldn't quite put a finger on it. I was living in a binary world. I was teaching these young people the history of the universe, which only someone with a defined Ego Centre could attempt to do in four months. So, while I was going through that process on one side, on the other side, for the first time in my life I had been introduced to esoteric writings.

It was my karma to end up with the three books of Alice Bailey, the so-called *Tibetan and Theosophical Society*, all of this 19th Century mystical astrology, this attempt to synthesise Christian and Hindu/Brahmin mysticism, and find a way to bring them all together. I was having difficulty with the language. It's just cumbersome language. I'm a man who likes things simple. I don't like convoluted people who are intoxicated with the exuberance of their own verbosity and don't take you anywhere at all. They just lead you around in circles and end up saying: "Well, if you're a student of the 'ninth level,' you're able to grasp this concept." However, there were these little nuggets, their take on the creation Program. I wasn't eating and I wasn't really sleeping. I was sleeping maybe two or three hours a night. I was aware of the fact that something was happening to me mechanically. It seemed like whole new areas of my mind were opening up to me. And it wasn't – that was the thing that was so odd about it – like it came from the exoteric or the esoteric. It was something about the quantum of that process. It was about what that awakened in *me*.

I think in many ways my intelligence had been conditioned and trained to be so exoteric that there was no balance, this blindness, not being able to see, not being able to see magic with every breath. It's the other side of seeing all the gears. So much of my process was shattering the arrogant, western intellectual and not replacing it with some kind of passive, oriental, yoga posture, but something else. It's about something else. For me, the thing that makes it interesting is that with every cycle something else happens. It's different. So, I was teaching these children and I was going through this long fast. And, of course, they obviously became aware of that.

I was already living on the property where I would ultimately have the experience with the Voice. But at the time, I was still living in the main house. There was a ruina behind the house, up above on another terrace. This ruina had one room which had been restored. It was ultimately in this room that I would have my extended "encounter". But at that time in that room was an English poet, a fellow by the name of Tim, who wrote good, solid 19th Century poetry and made beautiful butterflies that you could hang from your ceiling, which would go up and down. He was an interesting person. You could see him in the morning, sitting on the terrace in the lotus position doing Sanskrit chants. He'd been a personal assistant to Krishnamurti for a number of years, and lived with him both in India and in California. I'd given him a place to live.

On the eighth day of not eating, he came down. He was very concerned. He said to me that I could poison my system, that

I was a neophyte and I didn't know what I was doing. He insisted that I should stop my fast. I said to him: "I'm not fasting. I'm just not eating." It was a very different thing. Not that he grasped what I meant, but nonetheless. So, he said to me that he had made me up some kind of a herbal potion. He gave me this thing and told me to drink some of it with hot water a couple of times during the day. It would clean out my intestines. He was concerned about all this stuff that can build up in your body, and the toxins that are released when you stop eating. At that point, I hadn't eaten in eight days. And I didn't notice.

One of the things that's so interesting for me about hindsight and looking at my encounter with the Voice was, when I left North America, I weighed around 170 pounds. By the time I met the Voice, I weighed about 120 pounds. I've never weighed more than about 135 to 140 pounds since. My body went through a preparation. Basically, the fat of my body was something that was removed to a point that I looked like a "healthy Holocaust survivor", if that's possible to imagine. Later than what this story is about, I went through a fast for over six weeks. That's another space that one gets into, and I eventually got to see what I looked like, which was rather spooky. But this was my first experience. I had never known such a thing. I felt terrific. I felt no yearning, no loss. What I did notice was, I had more time. It was the thing that was so astonishing about the process. It was then that I realised how much time we spend thinking about shopping, preparing food, eating, cleaning up, shitting it out, and starting all over again. Endlessly. It's amazing how much time you have on your hands when you don't eat. It's really amazing.

Anyway, something obviously was very strange. Something was going on. We had entered into the Scorpion month. I had this friend of mine, truly a shaman, in many ways the epitome of a late 20th Century shaman, and a Scorpion. We had arranged a gathering of Bob, the Scorpion, myself and Frank to use ketamine. The three of us were going to meet at Frank's house. It was a classic Scorpion November. Incredibly dark, but full of light and spooky. The old dirt roads going through these orchards where the trees in the winter, in the shadow of the evening starlight, are really spooky. They're living sentinels. They look like a bad dream sometimes. I can remember the drive up to the house that night. It would forever change my life. It was Thanksgiving. And it turned out this *was* really my Thanksgiving. It was my "jumping-off-point place", about a whole transformation in how one can see and how it's brought to you. You can't go after it, you can't look for it, you can't hunt for it, and you can't even wait for it. Even waiting for it is insane. There's nothing to do. There's just breath. One breath after the other, and maybe, and maybe, and maybe—

I am obviously very lucky. What else to say about "no choice"?

So, the three of us met for this shamanistic experience of injecting ketamine. Later, Frank had gone off to go to sleep. Bob wasn't feeling well, and he had curled up in one of the corners near the fireplace. I was sitting there with my back to the fire. In front of me was one of these coffee tables, sort of a catchall. It was like a giant leather basket with all kinds of stuff thrown in there – books, pens, writing paper, stuff. So, I'm in this very beautiful finca in the countryside. There is a cat, and I'm sitting in the main room which is called an *entrada* and see this black cat go to the front door, wanting to get out. I don't feel like moving. This cat just starts to talk to me. It was an interesting moment. I go over, I open up the door, and I let the cat out, closing the door. I go back to the fire and sit down. Maybe after 15 minutes, just sitting there warming myself, just not focused on anything, the door opens. It just opens. These were heavy wooden doors, and I had closed the door. I had clearly closed the door because the night was cold. Still, the door opened. I figure, okay, maybe I didn't close it. So, I get up and go over to the door and I close the door again. I really make sure to close the door this time, go back to the fire and sit down.

I don't know how long it took, a few minutes, and the door opens up again. This time, when the door opens up I have two reactions. One is this common, the "hair standing up on the back of your neck" business. I get that as the first sensation. Then, very calmly, I watch the cat walk back into the house. When the cat walks back into the house, I suddenly get physical stomach cramps, very sharp. Sharp enough to make you say "Ouch!" It had been six days since I was given that potion that was supposed to instantaneously, within 24 hours, clean out my intestinal tract. Now, six days later, because it was too weak, all of a sudden I get this incredible cramping. I go into the bathroom in the house and I realise I don't want to be in that bathroom, so I grab a whole wad of toilet tissue and I go out this open door, out of the house.

In front of the house, to the right, is an orchard. Just as you enter into the orchard, there is an absolutely enormous olive tree, a beautiful thing. I go over to this olive tree, and I squat down under this olive tree to see if I can get rid of these cramps. As I'm sitting there, I can see a full Moon. The Moon is rising up over the house. So I'm looking out from underneath the night shadow of this olive tree, squatting there. The Moon is in front of me. It's incredible what can come out of your body. It was like black oil. It was amazing. After that process, I don't think I ever will be again as clean on the inside as I was through that process. As I'm going through this, and the Moon is rising, I hear something. It doesn't go away. I'm staring at the Moon while I'm going through this cramping process, and I'm hearing this sound. As I look at the Moon, I also hear a voice. It was distinctly a female voice. It said: "It sounds like an airplane." And that's exactly what it sounded like. It sounded like an airplane. But it sounded like an airplane that isn't coming any closer and isn't moving further away. There was no Doppler effect. There was just this very odd whine of sound of an airplane. And I can't get it out of my head. So I go through that process and I clean myself up. It was very cold.

I go back into the house and I close the door. I go sitting by the fire to warm up. I guess I get to sit there for about 10 minutes when the door opens and the cramps come back. So I go back, and I do exactly the same thing, all over again. The Moon is bigger, and it's higher in the sky. And there is this persistence of this sound. It was almost irritating. I cleaned myself up and again, I went back into the house, closing this door. I went to sit by the fire. As I'm sitting by the fire, I look into this basket in front of me, and I see these kinds of stationary store, cute, little books with blank pages that they sell without lines.

I remember pulling one out of the basket, and noticing that there was nothing in it. Nothing had been written in it.

There was a very beautiful pen. It just had a certain quality. It was golden, and I remember taking it in my hand. I don't know how to describe what happened next, because I wasn't there. I guess I blacked out. I don't know how that works. What I *do* know is that when I gained consciousness, or at least relative consciousness, back in the world I assumed I was in, that book was no longer empty. It had been filled up. As I turned the pages – there is no language to describe what it means to know something without understanding it. I don't know how to explain that – I can't. The book was filled with glyphs, numbers, shapes, words I did not know. People call that *automatic writing*. I don't know what to call it. It still remains for me one of those extraordinary mysteries, that there was my "vehicle" writing all of that stuff and my "passenger" was on vacation, totally out of the loop. Here was this incredible magical book. There were things that I had grasped without knowing what they were. It would take 10 years before I could actually consciously grasp some of those things that were there before me in that book. What was happening to me – I had no idea.

That book was very holy to me. It was my personal evidence that I had crossed over some kind of line. It had stopped being a subjective movie, and had become an objective experience. It was a very important step for my consciousness. It was evidence for me. For me only. It's not evidence for anyone else, it can't be. But for me it was evidence that there was an awful lot more to life, the way we see what's going on, the forces. Nobody has ever seen it. It's the magic of that little book. I woke up my friend and I said to him: "You're not going to believe this! You're not going to believe this! No one would believe this. You should see this. It's utter outer worldly, it's incredible!" He said to me: "What are you talking about? I just want to go to sleep, leave me alone!" I said: "You've got to see this!" He said: "I don't want to see it!" So I said: "Okay, you never will." About three months later I would burn it, but that's another story.

It was incredible. It was incredible, because I realised that there were things in it that were nowhere within my consciousness memory to have or associate with. It's like it was science fiction. Honest to God, absolutely incredible, first-class science-fiction. There was this mix in me of wonder, fear and excitement. It was amazing. It was almost like it was burning my hand as I held it. It was the first time that I got to see the mystery of the G, the folding of the cycle. Ah, the G is really something. It would take me so many years to grasp what I actually drew in that state in a simple image. It was amazing. These glyphs, the glyphs that you associate with juxtaposition and the Bases, there were all these things that were there. More than that, the odd thing was that, as strange as they were, I knew they were mine. They belonged, in that sense, to me. They were for me. This was not some kind of random "fax" that had been picked up. I realised that I had to look at my process with a different perspective. By the way, not that night.

So, I sat there with this little book in my hand, I would open it up, look at a page and then close it almost giggling. I don't know how to describe it. It's the kind of thing that happens to you when you're in a car accident, but you're not hurt and you laugh. I would look at those pages, and close them, and there would be this laughter, this surprise. It's a surprise. Ah, the surprise. There was no "where did this come from?" There was just this absolute surprise.

So, while I'm going through this process of spinning, the door opens up. There are things that happen that there's no rational way to understand them. There was no wind to open that door. Those doors were closed. I don't know what opened the door. It was part of the "shattering" for me. Maybe the door didn't open. Maybe I just saw it open and walked through it. I don't know. Because the moment that you are in an experience like that, you're in a bubble. The bubble is the magic. The magic isn't you. The serendipity of being in the bubble. Yeah, that's a treat, but it's the bubble, it's always the bubble. The door opens up. I don't have cramps finally, which was nice, they really hurt. There was a cloak that Frank wore, one of these heavy kinds of felt cotton cloaks with a hood.

Frank's a very big guy, much, bigger than me. Maybe 6'2" or 6'3" and big boned. So, it was a huge thing, and I was cold. I didn't want to be cold outside, so I reached over and grabbed this cloak, put it over my shoulders and put the hood over my head, going outside.

I didn't know what I was doing out there. I was just in the flow of the experience. I go outside and I go down the stairs. I realise that as I'm going down the stairs, I can see in incredible detail my shadow in front of me. You have to live in the countryside to know how incredible a Moon shadow can be.

There was this huge, full Moon that was there over my shoulders at this point. When I went to the bottom of the stairs, I turned around and I looked at the full Moon. The moment that I stood there, looking at the full Moon, I hear this sound again, this "airplane with no Doppler effect". I had already experienced wonder. I had already experienced excitement, but I wasn't ready for the fear.

It's exciting to break through, but then, where are you? You are not in any place that you know or understand anymore. Something took a hold of me physically, in the way in which an adult takes hold of a six-year old, clasps me with hands on either side of my forearms and shoulders, and turns me around. That's how it felt. It was a terrifying experience. I don't have any other way to describe that.

Fortunately, I had been on a long fast, because I tell you: just thinking about it now, reminds me of how spooky that was.

To be grabbed like that, and turned around. And then, something really odd happened. Simultaneously with the turning, I could hear roosters, dogs and horses and birds – all calling. Dogs barking, horses somewhere off in the distance neighing. And as I'm turned, I look to the east, to the horizon. What I see is the corona of the Sun beginning to emerge, this faint, just breaking of light. But within that, there's this hot, white spot. Hot, white spot – it was so beautiful – just at the edge of the horizon. And right beside is this tiny little smirch. When I see this hot spot and this thing beside it, I lose a normal sense of consciousness and sight. It was like being fed the way a strobe light works. But a strobe light that had many colours and was pattern rooted. It felt like I was being showered, almost in patterns, streaming patterns, streaming from that source. I don't imagine it lasted longer than a minute. To me, it seemed like eternity. I didn't know if I was going to survive. I had no grasp at all of what was happening to me. And I was still full of the adrenal rush of being grabbed and turned.

When it stopped, the Sun was full in the sky. This incredible fast jumping Sun at sunrise. And I hear Frank coming out of the house. He asked me what I was doing. I said to him:
"Do you hear it?"
"What?"
"Do you hear it?" – because the sound was so strong in my head.
It would take another three or four hours for that sound to go away.

What I saw on that horizon on that morning was the triple conjunction of the Sun, Mercury and Halley's Comet. It's one of those really odd, mystical encounters. I had never known that it was possible. I had mocked it, I had made fun of it, I had belittled it. It seemed to me that these stories, these fairy tales, these whatever – that they were not "truths". That somehow they were just a by-product of failed human psychology. I didn't believe in God or a godhead. I didn't have any of that. I was as close to narcissistic nihilism as anyone can be.

And then —boom! This one night in my life.
Everything that I thought of as the world disappeared.

It disappeared. In that moment, I no longer trusted anything, I couldn't.

I realised how blind people were, that they did not see that these forces were everywhere, and at work. My whole life changed, everything changed.

I began to die, literally. This intellectual, western being that I was, it all of a sudden began to die. Everything about my self no longer had any continuity with what I understood to be the potential of knowing. It all got shattered.

There were mysterious forces. I had encountered them. There is information that comes from someplace else. And you get it. You can be grabbed by the air and turned like a doll. With all my deep intellectuality, *that* was just overwhelming. And it was very frightening.

What are these forces? What do they want?

Do they want anything? What's going on?

This was the beginning of my journey to the Voice, where it truly began.

This is where I would break off completely with any connection to normal life.

I would just go wild and return to the source. Go to the source of the illusion – me – each of us.

It was something. I had to digest it.

I had to give up on the world. And I did.

I gave up on all of it.

It was all a lie.

It was all nonsense.

A world of blindness.

A world filled with nothing but delusion and delusion, supporting the delusions.

There are forces that turn you in the night. And here were all these beings, just trapped on the mundane plane, and I was this wild man up there in the hills.

I couldn't go back into that world. It seemed so profane, so dense, vulgar, and unclean.

I stopped eating, weeks and weeks and weeks. And I would sit and feed on the Sun. A strange thing.

There was a calming, as all of these stored things in my body slowly began to be leached out of me.

The deconstruction was complete.

I guess all of what happened was the beginning of my preparation for the Voice. I didn't know what was coming. I had no idea. At this point, I was just holding on for dear life. I had no idea what was going to happen. One simply can't. You can't... You get to the other side, and all the rules change.

Everything changes.

—Ra Uru Hu

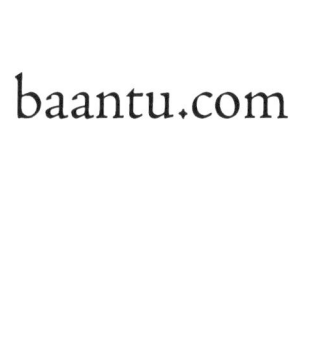

About the author

Steve Rhodes is the founder of BaanTu. He is a British musician, computer programmer, book author, and owner of a record company. Born in Austria, he studied mechanical engineering-management before moving to London. While at university, he won a nationwide search for best music-newcomer and subsequently got signed to CBS Records. Various TV, radio and other media appearances followed. Until 2010, Steve owned one of the leading recording studios in London, Alpha Centauri, which was used by U2, Kanye West, M.I.A., and Depeche Mode. His music can be heard at marquii.net.

Ra Uru Hu

Robert Alan Krakower (9 April 1948 – 12 March 2011) started to call himself Ra after he disappeared in 1983. He left behind his old life, work and family, who eventually declared him dead. In Canada, he had owned a media company that produced some of the first rock 'n roll videos as well as television commercials and fashion programs. After his disappearance, he ended up on the Mediterranean island of Ibiza where – after years of living wild with no money – he had a life-changing encounter in January 1987 with what he called "the Voice". It was the Voice that gave Ra the title, Uru Hu.

The Encounter 1
The Design of Humans 21
    The Crystals and the Monopole 23
    The Graph 27
    The Mandala Wheel 29
    The Flow of Information 31
    The Crystal Bundles and the Incarnation Process 33
    Human Conception 35
    Death 36
The Architecture of Life 39
The Story of the Consciousness Crystals 45
    The Bhan & Tugh and the Beginning of our Universe 47
    The Magic of Conception 51
    Fractal Lines and the Centre 52
    Neutrinos – the Breath of Stars 56
    Stars 58
    The Beginning Before the Start 59
    The Initiation of the Life Process 62
    The Centre 66
    The Camel and the Dog 67
    The Four Corners 72
    The Death of Sirius 76
    The Deterioration of the Yin/Yang 82
    The 16 Faces 86
    The 66 Sides 90
2027 and the Beyond 95
The Design of Raves 107
    The Autive Circuit 110
    The Autive Circuit's Stream of Telling 111
    The Autive Circuit's Stream of Taking 112
    The Gate of Access 112

The Experiential Circuit 116
The Collective Circuit 117
The Material Circuit 121
The Binary Circuit 127
The Individualistic Circuit 129
The Conscious Rave Penta 137
Global Cycles and a Brief History of the Round 145
The Precession of the Equinox 149
The Round of Civilisation – The Lock and the Key 150
The Cycle of the Sleeping Phoenix 154
The Apocalypse 161
The Night of Brahma 169
The Galilean Moon Europa 177
Oberon and the Reconstitution 181
The Eron 191
The Arrival of the Single Personality into the Totality 195
Epilogue 211
About the author 231
Ra Uru Hu 233

Printed in Great Britain
by Amazon